John Francis Waller

Festival Tales

John Francis Waller

Festival Tales

ISBN/EAN: 9783743330672

Manufactured in Europe, USA, Canada, Australia, Japa

Cover: Foto ©ninafisch / pixelio.de

Manufactured and distributed by brebook publishing software (www.brebook.com)

John Francis Waller

Festival Tales

FESTIVAL TALES

BY

JOHN FRANCIS WALLER,

AUTHOR OF "POEMS," "THE SLINGSBY PAPERS," ETC.

> "Pray you sit by us,
> And tell 's a tale,"
> "Tell o'er thy tale again."
>
> SHAKSPEARE.

DUBLIN:

M. H. GILL AND SON,
50 UPPER SACKVILLE-STREET.
1879.

PREFACE.

THE Tales of which this Volume is composed are selected from amongst a great many which, with one exception, appeared in various periodicals in England and Ireland. They had a reception sufficiently favourable to induce me to venture on their reproduction in the present form. I have made a few not very important changes in some of them, and have curtailed others, so as to give, I hope, a continuity to the whole.

The experiment of putting out these compositions for the second time is made not without some diffidence. The taste of the public has in many respects changed since their original appearance: what pleased once may not please again.

Two of the Tales, "Christmas Eve," and "Turned to the Wall," are now republished by the kind permission of Messrs. Cassell, Petter and Galpin.

JOHN FRANCIS WALLER.

CONTENTS.

	PAGE
NEW YEAR'S DAY.—Abraham Scrimble's Will	1
ST. VALENTINE'S DAY.—The Martyr	28
EASTER DAY.—St. Mary's-Super-Mare	74
ALL HALLOW EVE.—Snap-apple Night at Castle Slingby	99
THE FEAST OF ALL SOULS.—The Count of Castel Vecchio	131
CHRISTMAS EVE.—A Tale of Two Travellers	201
INNOCENTS' DAY.—Turned to the Wall	234
NEW YEAR'S EVE.—Snowed up—Balancing the Books	269

FESTIVAL TALES.

New Year's Day.

ABRAHAM SCRIMBLE'S WILL.

CHAPTER I.

HOW ALL THE SCRIMBLES MET IN OLD JEWRY, TO "HEAR SOMETHING TO THEIR ADVANTAGE."

ONE fine summer's day, in the year of our Lord 1853, there was assembled, in the chambers of Mr. Reuben Levi, in Old Jewry, in the city of London, the whole family of the Scrimbles, who had come up from Somersetshire upon the following invitation, which was advertised in the *Times* newspaper:—

"The next of kin of Abraham Scrimble, of Cincinnati, in the State of Ohio, America, and formerly of the county of Somerset, in England, lately deceased, are requested to attend at my chambers in No. 972B Old Jewry, on Monday, the 20th day of June next, at the hour of twelve o'clock, where they will hear of something to their advantage.

"Reuben Levi."

Well, sure enough, they were all there in wondering expectation. There was a tradition amongst the youngsters of the family about Abraham Scrimble. He had quarrelled with his father, and gone off, no one ever knew where, till the advertisement at once informed them of his death, and the place where he had resided. The clock of St. Paul's had scarcely struck twelve, when Mr. Levi, accompanied by another gentleman, entered the apartment where the Scrimbles were congregated.

"The next of kin of Mr. Abraham Scrimble, I presume?" said the man of law, making an œcumenical bow to the assembled Scrimbles.

"Yes, yes," was the response from a dozen voices, or thereabouts.

"Bless me," said the lawyer, "what a fortunate man Mr. Scrimble was to have so many next of kin!"

"Well, I don't know, I'm sure," said the other gentleman, drily, "but we shall see. Pray proceed to business, Mr. Levi."

"Gentlemen and ladies," said that gentleman, examining a paper, "I find that the late Mr. Abraham

Scrimble had, when he left this country, two sisters and one brother."

"So he had," said one of the company; "there was his brother Ebenezer, my father—he is dead, and left five of us;" and with a sweep of his hand the speaker indicated his two brothers and two sisters.

"Very good," said the man of law; "you are, then, next of kin in the fourth degree. Well, then, Kezia was the name of one of his sisters, wasn't it?"

"Oh, yes; Kezia was his eldest sister."

"Is she living or dead?"

"Dead as a door nail."

"Good, again," said Mr. Levi. "Did she leave any issue?"

"I should hope not," was the reply, "seeing that she was never married; and, up to the last hour of her life—and she lived to be over seventy—she maintained the reputation of being an immaculate old maid."

"In that case, sir," said Mr. Levi, turning to the other gentleman, "Aunt Kezia is clean out of the way—an unfruitful branch in the family tree. We will write her down as *Ob. S. P.*"

"And what may that mean?" asked one of the next of kin.

"Oh, that's a short way we have of stating that she died without issue."

"If that's all, you may write it down with a safe conscience."

And Mr. Levi accordingly jotted down the letters *Ob. S. P.* after Aunt Kezia's name.

"Now, what about the other sister?"

"That was my mother, Dorcas," said another member of the family; "she married her own cousin-german."

"Just so," said Mr. Levi; "I have it all here."

"Have you?" said the other. "Well, then, maybe you have something about me there, too?"

"Maybe I have. Who are you?"

"I'm the *consequence* of that auspicious union—Jacob Scrimble, at your service."

"And your father and mother?"

"Dead these fifteen years."

"Your brothers and sisters, are they alive?"

"No."

"Dead, too?"

"No. They ain't dead, because they never were alive; and they ain't alive, because they never were born—I was an only child."

"Ah! I understand: well, you are another next of kin in the fourth degree."

"I'm a cousin-german of old Abraham," said a little man, of about fifty years of age; "I'm a son of his uncle Amos, and the rest of his children died very young."

"Then," replied the man of law, "you are also related to the deceased in the fourth degree. And now as to all the rest?"

"Oh, they're distant relations—fortieth cousins, as the saying is, and have just come to keep us company."

The investigation of kindred having been thus concluded, the other gentleman advanced to the table, and taking from the breast-pocket of his coat a packet, he opened it with great formality, and thus addressed the company:—

"Ladies and gentlemen of the Scrimble family, I hold in my hand the last will and testament of my deceased friend, the late Abraham Scrimble. He died some three months since in the town of Cincinnati, full of years, and not empty of cash. As one of his executors, I shall now read you the part of his will which concerns you. '*Item*—As it was the will of God that I should quarrel with my father, and leave my native land before my brothers and sisters were grown up to quarrel with, and having no issue of my own to leave my money to, and not knowing what relatives I have in England, I bequeath the sum of five thousand dollars to whichever of my next of kin shall first attain the age of twenty-one years after my decease, and make proof of his having attained his majority, before either of my executors, or the proper authority of the place where he shall be resident at the time. And the residue of my worldly goods and substance I leave as follows.' But that does not concern the present company," said Mr. Hucklebones, refolding the paper, and redepositing it in his pocket. "And now, Mr. Levi, be so good, pray, as to inform us who is to get the five thousand dollars?"

"Why, Mr. Hucklebones, here are the next of kin—Ebenezer's five children. Pray, what are your names?"

"I'm Esau, the eldest; then there is ——"

"What's your age?"

"I'm twenty; and I'll be twenty-one the first day of January next, of all days in the year."

"Well, then, we needn't ask anything about your brothers or sisters. Kezia is out of the way, and next comes Mr. Jacob, Dorcas's only child. Pray, what may your age be, Mr. Jacob?"

"The same as cousin Esau's to a day. The brother and sister had a run for it, you see."

"Ay, cousin Jacob, but you know I was born three hours before you."

"That's no matter," said Mr. Levi, "'*de minimis non curat lex;*' the law takes no account of such trifles as a few hours. You will both be of age the same moment—the very instant after the clock strikes twelve at night on the 31st of December next."

"This is a very strange case," said Mr. Hucklebones; "it strikes me that neither of these young gentlemen will be entitled to the legacy, or that they should divide it."

"They cannot divide it," said the lawyer. Two women sometimes may make one heir, being, I suppose, considered as equal only to one man; but there can no more be two males entitled to one property than two suns in the heavens, Mr. Hucklebones. Therefore I think this is a '*casus omissus;*' and in such case ——"

"In such a case the money comes to me, Gideon Scrimble," said the elderly cousin, "as you say I am also one of the next of kin."

"Well, so you are. But when do you expect to attain your age of twenty-one, Mr. Gideon?"

"Oh, he's been and done it nigh thirty years ago," said Esau, chuckling.

"So much the better—ain't it?" retorted Gideon. "I've performed the condition beforehand, and am ready to receive the money this instant."

"I should rather think, sir," said Mr. Hucklebones, "that you have run a long chalk beyond the winning-post, and at the wrong side of it, too; and before you can get back again, some of these young folks will have come up and won the race."

"Just so," said Mr. Levi; "Mr. Gideon is quite out of the question; he will never attain the age of twenty-one in his present state of existence, and time, Mr. Hucklebones, is 'of the essence of the contract,' as the lawyers say; and therefore I am disposed to consider this as a case of a lapsed legacy, and the money must sink into the residue, and go to the Cosmopolitan Ragged College of Cincinnati."

All the next of kin of Abraham Scrimble, deceased, looked dismayed at this announcement. They would have gladly come to any compromise so as to divide the bone amongst them, rather than that it should be picked by a transatlantic academy of half-naked Yankee boys. At last Jacob said—

"The money is to be given to the person who shall first reach twenty-one—ain't it?"

"Yes, just so."

"Well, then, we must all wait awhile. Who can tell which of us will be first of age; I may die, or Esau, or both, and then one of the others would step into our places."

"Upon my word, that's very true. Mr. Hucklebones, we were overlooking that fact altogether."

"I think so," said the executor; "we are all premature. I therefore propose that we all assemble here half-an-hour before midnight on the last day of the year, and we shall then be in a condition to decide who shall be entitled to the legacy. Are you agreed, ladies and gentlemen?"

A general assent was given, whereupon Mr. Hucklebones bowed himself out of the room, and Mr. Levi bowed out all the next of kin of Abraham Scrimble, late of Cincinnati, in the State of Ohio, deceased.

CHAPTER II.

HOW ESAU SCRIMBLE TOOK TIME BY THE FORELOCK.

THE great clock of St. Paul's had pealed out the half-hour before midnight upon the last day of December, 1853, when Mr. Reuben Levi again entered his chambers in Old Jewry, accompanied as before by Mr. Hucklebones, the executor of the late Mr. Abraham Scrimble, of Cincinnati.

"Happy to see you all, ladies and gentlemen," said the man of law.

"All alive and well, I see," said Mr. Hucklebones. "Ah, Mr. Esau, I see you are not likely to die before you come of age, and so give either of your pretty sisters there a chance. Mr. Gideon, your humble servant; have you made much lee-way against the stream of time since last I had the pleasure of seeing you? How much *under* fifty may you be by this?"

Gideon was about to return a snappish reply to this *mauvaise plaisantrie*, when Mr. Hucklebones suddenly exclaimed—

"Bless my soul, where is Mr. Jacob; nothing has happened to him, I hope?"

"Well, I don't know," said Esau; "he suddenly disappeared about a fortnight ago, at which time he was in excellent health and spirits; but none of us have since heard or seen anything of him."

"How strange!" said Mr. Levi. "Did you advertise for him in the public papers?"

"Why, no," said Esau; "we had no particular interest in bringing him here to-night, you know; but we drained out the fish-pond at Scrimbleton, and had the river dragged, but he didn't turn up in either."

"Very strange, indeed, and I must say very mysterious, too!" said the man of law, with a lowering countenance.

"Ah, poor fellow!" said Mr. Hucklebones, "do you remember the observation which he made when we were all here last summer—'I may die, or Esau,' said he. 'Tis very strange, indeed—very strange; I hope his words may not turn out true as to himself."

"Well," said Mr. Levi, "now to business, as time is precious. Since our last meeting I have made all necessary searches, and find the pedigree of the family has been stated correctly. It seems to me, therefore, that the only person who will be in a condition to claim this legacy is Mr. Esau Scrimble, supposing that anything has happened to his cousin Jacob, which I confess I have much reason, from the peculiar circumstances of the case, to fear;" and again the lawyer looked loweringly at Esau. "Are you prepared, sir, to prove, by a certificate attested by the proper authority—I mean when the time comes—your age of twenty-one?"

"Certainly, sir. Here is a copy of the registry of my birth, and it is duly certified and signed by the rector of the parish, and by Squire Bolderly, the nearest justice of the peace. Be so good as to see that it is all right."

"Put up the paper, put it up, sir, please, for the present," said Mr. Levi coldly, thrusting back the proffered document. "The time is not yet come—many a slip between the cup and the lip, Mr. Esau. Who knows but your poor cousin Jacob may arrive before midnight."

"Well, maybe he may, Mr. Levi," replied Isaac, with an incredulous toss of his head; "I've no doubt he will, if he's anywhere within the British dominions. Jacob was always a wide-awake fellow, and just the man not to neglect the main chance."

At this moment there was a loud knock at the door of the outer chamber, that made every one start, and Esau turn pale. Mr. Levi's clerk opened the door, and ushered a man muffled up in a cloak into the inner department. The man took off his cloak very deliberately, and then sat down, after which he took his watch from his fob, and looked at the hour, and said—

"11, 43′ 22″."

"May I ask, sir," said Mr. Levi, "your business?"

"Oh," said Mr. Hucklebones, "I'll tell you what brings him here. This is Mr. Pinionwheel, the great chronometrician. You know, Mr. Levi, you said, 'time was of the essence of the contract,' and so I thought it best to have the highest living authority upon that point, and I requested Mr. Pinionwheel to attend here to-night, to keep a sharp look out upon the time."

"I can't sufficiently admire your forethought, sir," said the lawyer, with as near an approach to a smile as he ever allowed his features the relaxation of indulging in. "Pray, sit down, Mr. Pinionwheel."

That gentleman took his seat, and the next instant the clock of Saint Paul's told the third quarter.

"Right, within three seconds," said Mr. Pinion-wheel, again consulting his watch.

"While we are waiting, Mr. Hucklebones," said one of the fortieth cousins, "perhaps you will be so kind as to tell us something about our deceased relative. Did he leave much property?"

"A pretty considerable amount, sir—something over 200,000 dollars."

"How much may that be of our money?"

"Well, near £50,000."

"Indeed—and did he leave no bequests to his relatives in general—nothing to buy mourning-rings, you know?"

"Not a cent."

"And who gets all these dollars, may I ask, sir?"

"Oh, certainly: he left 1000 dollars to Lilly, and 1000 dollars to Snowball, besides giving each of the girls her freedom—remarkably nice niggers they are—twenty dollars to each slave on the estate, a trifle of 10,000 dollars each to myself and my co-executor, and the residue to the Cosmopolitan Ragged School of Cincinnati."

"I suppose, sir, the will is all regular?"

"Well, I'm sure I don't know; but Mr. Levi can answer that question, I suppose."

"All right and formal," said the gentleman appealed

to. "The duplicate is in my possession, and may be inspected by any member of the family of Scrimble. Here it is, gentlemen."

The lawyer spread the will on the table, and the company amused themselves reading it over, by way of passing the time. It was a hopeless investigation; there was not a cent, as Mr. Hucklebones said, left to any of the Scrimbles, except the 5000 dollars; and there was not a flaw in the document, not a blot, nor an erasure; and at the foot was the testator's name, in big, sturdy, independent characters, with a dash at the end, as much as to say, "There's the handwriting of a man of sound and disposing mind, memory, and discretion, who knows what he's about, and doesn't care a straw who is pleased or who isn't, by jingo!" And so time sped on, when Mr. Hucklebones, addressing Mr. Pinionwheel, said—

"Pray, sir, what may the hour be?"

"Eleven hours, fifty-eight minutes, forty-three seconds, Greenwich time," said the horologer, oracularly.

"Coming pretty close up to time, Mr. Esau," remarked the executor.

"In less than two minutes more, you'll cease to be an infant, sir," added the lawyer, and then ——"

"Rat! tat! tat! tat!! A furious peal at the outer

door. The clerk sprang from the high stool in the office, where he had just gone off in a doze, and in one bound he was at the door. A young man rushed in breathless, and then looking at his watch, said—

"It just wants one minute yet of twelve o'clock."

"Less by two seconds, sir," said Mr. Pinionwheel, authoritatively, after having examined his timekeeper.

"Oh! hang your two seconds!" cried the stranger, impatiently. "Mr. Levi, allow me to introduce myself to you, sir—Mr. Lynxley, sir, at your service—junior partner of the firm of Swift and Lynxley, Clifford's Inn."

"Pray be seated, my dear sir," said Mr. Levi, handing his brother chip a chair. "May I ask to what I am indebted for the honour of this visit at such an unseasonable—at least, such an unbusiness-like hour? I may say it is now midnight."

"And no mistake," added Esau Scrimble; "for there goes the clock of Saint Paul's."

And accordingly the heavy strokes of the hour were pealed out one by one from old Saint Paul's clock-tower, falling, as it were, upon the startled ear of the sleeping city, and telling that swarming hive of human beings that they had now entered upon another year of existence.

CHAPTER III.

HOW TIME LEFT ESAU SCRIMBLE IN THE LURCH.

There was a profound silence in the inner chamber of Mr. Reuben Levi during the short space in which Old Time, with his iron tongue, was registering the momentous point in his progress which we have just indicated.

When the reverberation of the last clang had died away among the dusty books on the cobwebbed shelves, Esau Scrimble rose up, and stepping forward to the table at which Mr. Hucklebones was sitting, thus addressed the executor:—

"I have now, sir, the honour to lay before you the formal proofs of my having at this present moment attained the age of twenty-one years. Here is a copy taken from the registry kept in the parish church of Scrimbleton-on-the-Hill, duly attested by Parson Smithson and Squire Bolderly. You will see it is quite satisfactory."

The executor of the will of Abraham Scrimble, deceased, took the document, and read it over slowly and carefully. He then handed it to Mr. Levi, who likewise having read it, asked—

"Can you prove that these signatures are in the handwriting of the Parson and the Squire?"

"Oh! that's easily done; I can depose to the fact myself, and so can Naomi here, and so can Ruth, and so can Joash, and so can ——"

"That will do—that will do," said Mr. Levi; "show them the document, please."

The paper passed through the hands of all the Scrimbles there assembled, who, with one accord, pronounced the signatures to be genuine. The executor and his legal adviser now consulted together for a moment, and then Mr. Hucklebones said—

"The proof seems quite satisfactory, Mr. Esau; and you would, of course, be entitled to the legacy under my deceased friend's will, if there were any certainty that no other claimant would come forward. It is however, quite possible that your cousin Jacob may yet make his appearance, and you know that he attained his majority at the same moment as yourself."

"Well, and suppose that he did, and suppose that he does turn up, still I am entitled to the legacy as having *first* made the proper proof of having attained my majority. I have taken legal advice upon the words of the will, and am assured that such is their true construction. Will you be so good, Sir, as to read them?"

Mr. Hucklebones read the words—"I bequeath to

whichever of my next of kin shall first attain the age of twenty-one years, after my decease, and make proof of his having attained his majority, before either of my executors, or the proper authority of the place where he shall be resident at the time."

"Well, Mr. Levi, what do you say as to this point of law?"

"Upon my word, Mr. Hucklebones, I think there's something in it, Sir. Pray, Mr. Esau, may I ask whose opinion you have taken?"

"Certainly, Sir; I have taken the opinion of Mr. Beetle, and here it is."

"A very sound opinion, Sir, is Mr. Beetle," said the man of law, perusing the paper. "He is certainly quite in favour of your construction of the clause, Mr. Esau. Mr. Lynxley, may I ask you to look at this, and tell me what you think?"

Mr. Lynxley took the case, and, having cast his eye over it, said—

"I should not, of course, presume to put my opinion in competition with Mr. Beetle's, under any circumstances; but I confess I am strongly disposed to think he is right. I have seen a similar opinion of Mr. Perker upon the same point."

"Very good," said Esau, "I am quite contented to abide by the opinions of the legal gentlemen here present, Mr. Hucklebones, and I trust you will be guided by them, too."

Mr. Hucklebones was about to reply, when Mr. Lynxley interrupted him.

"Your pardon, my dear Sir, for a moment. Permit me now to explain to you and Mr. Levi how I happen to be here at what he very properly calls an unseasonable hour. I come on behalf of my client, Mr. Jacob Scrimble. May I request, Mr. Hucklebones, that you will have the goodness to look at this document."

Mr. Lynxley placed in the hands of the executor a paper which the latter read first to himself, and then aloud :—

"This is to certify that Mr. Jacob Scrimble, of Scrimbleton, in the County of Somerset, and Kingdom of England, comes now before me, and produces a certain paper writing which is now proved by two faithworthy witnesses here present to be a true copy of the original certificate of the baptism of the said Jacob Scrimble, deposited in the parish church of Scrimbleton-upon-the-Hill, whereby it appears that the said Jacob Scrimble has now attained his full age of twenty-one years. Given under my hand and seal of office, this first day of January, 1854, at one minute past twelve o'clock, P. M.

"Prefect of the Seine, Paris.

"*Present*—
    "DICKON GRUBB,
    "DOBBIN BUMBLE,
"Both of Scrimbleton-on-the-Hill,
    yeomen."

Mr. Huckleboncs laid down the paper, and stared silently at Mr. Levi, and Mr. Levi stared at Mr. Lynxley. Then everybody stared at Esau, and Esau stared at everybody. At length Esau broke the silence, and exclaimed vehemently—

"'Tis a forgery, an impossibility, and as such I denounce it."

"My good Sir, 'tis neither the one nor the other," replied Mr. Lynxley, with a sort of triumphant calmness. "That it is not a forgery, I will prove to the satisfaction of the gentlemen here when the original certificate shall arrive from Paris by the next mail. Neither is it an impossibility, inasmuch as I received it not ten minutes since at the Electric Telegraph Office."

"Well, and suppose you did," replied Esau; "I insist the document must have been ante-dated."

"Oh, don't imagine it," said Mr. Lynxley, with the same provoking calmness; "Mr. Jacob has managed matters too well for that. You will find it will turn out accurate to the minute."

"Gammon!" said Esau. "Will you tell me that what was written on the 1st of January, 1854, in Paris, could reach London on the 31st of December, 1853?"

"Oh, dear, yes," said Mr. Lynxley. "I'll tell you how 'twas all arranged, for I had the pleasure of leaving everything in train when I left Paris this, or rather yesterday, morning. You are all aware, gentlemen, that there is a difference of ten minutes between Paris and London time."

"No!" said Mr. Pinionwheel, emphatically, "9', 21", 28."

"Oh, bother!" said Mr. Lynxley, impatiently; "'tis all the same thing. Well, when the clock at the Telegraph Office in Paris struck twelve on the night of the 31st of December—the certificate was proved before the Prefect of the Seine, who was kind enough to attend there for the purpose—the message was then despatched on the instant—I had a cab all ready at the Lothbury office of the company, and received the despatch just in time to reach this before twelve o'clock."

"Well, then," said Esau, "even suppose so, I was before Jacob with my proof. His certificate is dated one minute after twelve. I made my proof the moment after the clock struck."

"Yes," said Mr. Lynxley, "Jacob's proof was then complete. Are you quite sure you did not take two minutes in making yours? But he must have been before you, for I had the evidence of it in my pocket here before you produced your certificate."

"If so, then, Jacob was too soon."

"No; you were too late."

"Jacob wasn't of age at the time."

"Not if he were in London; but he was in Paris."

"We both came of age the same moment."

"Pardon me—Jacob went to Paris to be of age before you."

"Fudge! Then, at that rate, if I went to Jericho, I should have been of age before him."

"Decidedly; but you didn't, you know, and that makes all the difference."

Esau was fairly driven into a corner, and didn't know what further to say. Mr. Lynxley turned to the executor, and his adviser, and drawing from his pocket-book a paper, he read as follows:—

"Gentlemen, in the name of my client, Mr. Jacob Scrimble, I now demand the legacy of 5000 dollars, bequeathed by the will of Abraham Scrimble, deceased, to which he claims to be entitled, under the terms of the said will; and I hereby caution you against paying the said sum, or any portion thereof, to any other person or persons, except to the said Jacob Scrimble, or his attorney, lawfully authorised thereto."

And as he so spoke, Mr. Lynxley handed the paper to Mr. Hucklebones with a polite bow.

"Well," said Mr. Hucklebones, "I'm blest if this ain't the queerest business I ever was engaged in during all my life. That Mr. Jacob is about the most go-ahead fellow in all creation, I calculate. He has gone a-head of old Father Time himself, and run slick into the new year before him. What am I to do, Mr. Levi?"

"Upon my word, my dear Sir," said the gentleman appealed to, "I think the only safe course for you will be to retain the money, and let the parties take the opinion of a court of equity. 'Tis a very nice question; ain't it, Mr. Lynxley?"

"Oh, very nice, *indeed*," said the latter gentleman, rubbing his hands together with manifest pleasure.

"I am under the guidance of my legal adviser," said Mr. Hucklebones, "and must decline to pay any of the claimants, whom I leave to their legal remedies."

"I'll spend the last shilling I have in the world," said Esau, "rather than suffer myself to be tricked out of my rights in this way."

"*Tricked!* did you say, Mr. Esau?" asked Mr. Lynxley, with very peculiar emphasis. "Who played the first trick, Sir? Who took advantage of a needy cousin's poverty, and induced him to leave the country, upon a solemn promise not to return till after the expiration of the year that is just past? And what did you give your cousin Jacob, Sir? Why, just £50 in hand, and a bond for £50 more, to be paid upon this day, provided he fulfilled the conditions you imposed upon him. Well, Sir, he has fulfilled the conditions; he is still in Paris, and I have his instructions to request the payment of this bond (and he exhibited the instrument to Esau) within four-and-twenty hours."

"I'll be hanged if I do," said Esau, in a rage. "He has not kept the terms of the agreement, as in honour bound."

"Honour!" said Lynxley, with a sneer. "Then, Sir, I shall be under the disagreeable necessity of taking legal steps to enforce payment. And so, gentlemen, I wish you all a good morning, and a happy new year." And Mr. Lynxley bowed to the company, and retired.

Gideon Scrimble now came forward, and said—

"Mr. Hucklebones, I beg to give you notice that I do not withdraw my claim to the legacy of my late worthy cousin Abraham. And though I have said little, I have thought all the more; and I have made up my mind to be at you as well as the rest. And so I wish you a good morning, and a happy new year." And Gideon retired upon the heels of Mr. Lynxley.

Then Mr. Hucklebones and Mr. Levi arose, and the latter took the various papers which had been laid on the table, and folded them carefully up, and put them in a tin box, labelled "Scrimble's Executors," and locked the box, and put the key in his pocket. And then he and Mr. Hucklebones politely bowed out all the kin Scrimble; and as they went down stairs, Esau could hear the executor and his lawyer indulging in low, chuckling laughter, as if they thought the whole transaction one of the finest jokes in the world.

But it was no joke, at least to some of the parties. Mr. Lynxley forthwith sued Esau upon the bond at law, and Esau obtained an injunction in equity to restrain Jacob from levying the amount. The executor very shortly after went back to Cincinnati, having arranged the private affairs that brought him to England. Esau forthwith instituted a suit in the courts at Cincinnati, to recover the legacy of old Abraham, and not having any favourable opinion of Yankee jurisprudence, he went over to superintend the warfare personally. Seeing this, Jacob took alarm, and did the same. Gideon would, no doubt, have followed them both, but unfortunately he was struck down by a fit of apoplexy just after he had packed up all his moveables. They put, by his own desire, "50" upon his coffin-plate, but it is strongly suspected that he was at least five years older, and the mistake can only be accounted for upon the supposition that he was constantly endeavouring to make lee-way against Time, as Mr. Hucklebones facetiously expressed it, in the hope that he might ultimately get back to one-and-twenty; and so he surely would, and in a very few years, at the rate of retrogression just mentioned, had not Death stepped in to the aid of outraged Time, and thus marred the ingenious scheme, as he does many another, and will do, as long as there is a schemer in the world subject to the laws of mortality. The contest was thus reduced to the single point, so strangely raised between Esau and Jacob. The lawyers of Esau were confident of success. The lawyers of Jacob said it was impossible he could fail. Mr. Hucklebones' lawyer was of opinion that neither Esau nor Jacob could claim the legacy, and that it fell into the residue. This opinion having been communicated to the Governor and Trustees of the Cosmopolitan Ragged College of Cincinnati, they forthwith gave their lawyer instructions to intervene in the suit, and put forward their claim, and so he did without a moment's delay. Thus the great suit of *Scrimble* v. *Scrimble* was constructed. It went on merrily—so far as the lawyers were concerned—and acrimoniously, as regarded the litigants; there was plenty of ink-shedding, and plenty of dollar-shedding too; the lawyers were incessantly opening their mouths in court; and the clients as frequently obliged to open their purses out of court. The counsel for Esau contended that the question of priority of birth was purely a question of fact. The counsel for Jacob contended it was purely a question of law. The counsel for the Cincinnati Ragged College insisted it was a mixed question of law and fact. The Court decided upon sending an issue to a jury, "Whether Esau, the plaintiff, or Jacob, the defendant, first attained the age of twenty-one years?" The jury returned a verdict, "That Esau, the plaintiff, and Jacob, the defendant, attained their age of twenty-one years at the same moment." Thereupon the Cincinnati Ragged College claimed the judgment of the Court in their favour, and the Court gave judgment accordingly. From this judgment the plaintiff appealed, and the cause was transferred to the Supreme Court of Appeal at Washington. How it has fared there has not as yet been announced to the rest of the kin Scrimble residing in Somersetshire. Each party reports with great confidence as to his own prospect of ultimate success; and, in fact, the matter has caused a very pretty schism amongst the Scrimbles, one party ranging themselves with Esau, and the other with Jacob; the consequence of which is, that the family never meet at the usual festival gatherings of Christmas or Easter without going to loggerheads upon the question. On one point alone are both Esauites and Jacobites fully agreed—namely, that whichever of the litigants shall succeed, he will not be a dollar the better of the legacy of old Abraham Scrimble, of Cincinnati, in the State of Ohio, in America.

St. Valentine's Day.

THE MARTYR.

CHAPTER I.

MOONLIGHT in the city! What a striking and solemnizing sight; how suggestive of thoughts that daylight never stirs within us. Life locked for a season in the arms of Death! The stony giant lies outstretched before us, snatching from the turmoil and excitement of day a short repose, to invigorate him for the same ever-recurring and ever-wasting turmoil and excitement to which the first ray of morning awakes him. The wanderer in the silent street hears the echoes of his own footfalls, where a few hours before the tread of a thousand steps, the rush, the roar, the struggle of life, stunned and distracted him. Houses gleam, silent and bleak, in the pale, cold light from which, in day, the tide of animation incessantly pours out upon the thoroughfares of existence. Not a throb without tells that the pulse of life is beating, but the blood has flowed back upon the heart of the city, as though it lay in a trance. Grief and joy, passion, avarice, and ambition, all seem at rest amid the scenes where, by day, they reign and revel.

> "Ships, towers, domes, theatres, and temples lie
> Open unto the fields and to the sky,
> All bright and glittering in the smokeless air."

The calm breath of night comes with renovating freshness upon the brow, as if it stole in from the pure country upon the unguarded slumber of the city, unpolluted with the reeking vapours, and smoke, and steam of the thronging human hive.

> "The river glideth at his own sweet will:
> Dear God! the very houses seem asleep,
> And all that mighty heart is lying still."

Moonlight in Rome! Who that has seen it may forget it ever? The Rome of our own time should so be seen. The garish sunlight suits not best the spectral city. She is a city of past memories, of faded glories, of devastated grandeur. And so—if you would rebuild her shattered walls, rear up her prostrate columns, restore her ruined fanes, and renovate her palaces—wander through her regions when the moon is at the full, that the things and beings of to-day may not mar your spirit as it goes back into the past. Then will Rome the Imperial arise before you; then will you truly understand how, though she be fallen from her high estate, and shorn of her world-wide dominion, still she is Rome the Eternal. Eternal in her glorious memories; Eternal in her influences upon all nations, for all share in the borrowed light of her arts, her wisdom, her learning, and her laws; Eternal in her history, which yet fills the foreground of the world's annals.

It was midnight, a few days before the Ides of February, in the year of the City 1023, and the 270th of the Redemption. The moon was then nigh its full, and poured down in a flood of mild and luminous glory upon the peerless city of Rome—the Rome of the Cæsars—ere the Goth or the Vandal had sacked her palaces, or kings of Christendom, more destructive than the Barbarians, filched away her precious monuments, her marbles, and her statuary; ere the fury of the Bourbon swept away in a desolating tide over all that Alaric and Genseric had spared, that Charlemagne and Robert of Sicily had left uninjured.

Passing along that portion of the Suburra that lay between the Esquilian and Cœlian Hills, a figure, wrapped closely in the coarse woollen toga which was worn by the meaner citizens, wended his cautious way northwestward, till he stood before the Flavian Amphitheatre, in later times known as the Colosseum. It was a sight that at such a moment might arrest the attention of the most indifferent or the most pre-occupied. Of this latter, it would seem, was he who now checked his steps, and flung from off his head the portion of his gown which had been drawn from his right shoulder so as to form the ordinary substitute for the *pileus*. The act disclosed a head singularly venerable; a few scant locks of long, white hair flowed down from the back portion along his neck: save these, the head was bald. A face, strongly marked and stern, bore traces of the grief and suffering which the conflict of powerful feelings with controlling principles ever leaves on the features; but his eye was still keen, black, and full of animation. On the first glance you would have pronounced him old, but a second look would have assured you he was old before his time, and had seen many sorrows and trials.

The old man threw back from his head the lappet of his gown, and gazed long and intently upon the pile before him. It was a glorious sight, that stupendous mass of buildings, as it then stood in all its integrity.

An oval of the most graceful form and magnificent dimensions, covering an area of ground as extensive as that upon which the largest pyramid of Egypt reposes, and faced with travertina stone, rose to the height of more than a hundred and fifty feet. The four stories of which it was composed exhibited each order of architecture in their proper succession, the basement being the severe Doric, the upper the florid and graceful composite, surmounted by an attic. The light of the moon, falling slantly athwart the face of the building, exhibited a chequered superficies of light and shade, whose picturesque effect could not be surpassed. In the ground story, the open archways, or vomitories, which, to the number of eighty, gave access at equal distance all round to the interior, were filled, some wholly, some partially, with the moonlight, according to the aspect they presented to the planet, and some lay buried in deep, black darkness; and so in the two succeeding stories, the light, as it fell upon the corresponding arches, displayed, more or less, the huge statues, to which they served as niches; and as the shadows of the projecting columns which sustained the entablatures crossed the forms or played flickering upon the massive features, when light clouds passed athwart the moon, the stone seemed endued with life, as if realizing the fabled story of Pygmalion. Spectral and cold, they stood in their places, and it required no stretch of fancy to believe them the ghosts of those who, within the area of this beautiful circus, had fought and bled, and died in a savage and unprovoked conflict with their fellow-men, or had fallen beneath the lacerating jaws of furious beasts.

Something of this sort appeared to cross the mind of the man, as his eye in its circuit passed along those marble effigies, whose features, as the shadows stirred along them, seemed at that moment trembling and twisting, as with the contortions of suffering. A spasm as of pain passed along his brow, and his lip quivered as he spoke in low emphatic tones of passion:—

"Oh, drunken—drunken with the blood of saints and of martyrs! What marvel if their mangled bodies be suffered to haunt the scenes of their slaughter, and to testify against their murderers, as their souls cease not, day and night, to cry to God for vengeance on those who have spilled their righteous blood. Yea, the very gore-soaked stones might cry aloud against them and thee, thou den of unclean beasts! How long, O Lord! holy and true, dost thou not judge and avenge our blood on them that dwell on the earth!"

The old man shook his hand denouncingly; and his utterance was choked with passion. In a moment, however, and by a violent effort, he mastered his feelings, and looking sorrowfully up to heaven, he struck his breast, and cried—

"'Miserere mei, Domine.' Have mercy upon me, O Lord! miserable sinner that I am! Who am I that I should invoke Thy wrath, to whom vengeance alone belongeth? Father, it may be that Thou reservest this place for a vessel of mercy and not of wrath. Haply, when the earth shall be filled with the knowledge of Thee, as the waters cover the sea, that the cross of Thy dear Son may be planted in this unholy circus, and the life-blood of Thy martyrs be worn away from its pavement by the feet of pilgrims and the knees of supplicating thousands. Even so, Lord, let it be, if it is Thy will."

The Christian bowed his head with a sigh, and reverently making the sign of the cross on his forehead, drew the lappet again over his head, and proceeded upon his solitary walk. Skirting the southern and western circuit of the Flavian amphitheatre, the old man passed on through the small archway for foot passengers in the eastern portion of the Arch of Constantine, and reached the space before the Temple of Venus and Rome. But the solitary paused not to contemplate the scene before him, but, with a passing glance, pursued his mission. Yet well might that scene win more than a passing glance. Raised on its ample platform, and reached at each angle by a flight of marble steps, between which rose a stately colonnade of white pillars, stood the Temple, its fluted Corinthian columns of Parian marble supporting a roof sheeted with bronze-gilt tiles, which caught the pale, modest rays of the moon, and sent them back blushing and ruddy from the rude, ungenial contact. Close to the Temple stood the colossal figure of bronze, one hundred and twenty feet high, from which the head of Nero had been removed to make way for that of Apollo, now radiant with mimic sunbeams, while nearer to the Arch of Constantine spread the spacious basin of the Meta Sudans. A fair and a tranquillizing sight was it to look upon the jet of plenteous and pure water that flung itself out of the high conical fountain upwards into the clear moonlight sky, and then disparting circularly in every direction as it reached its highest elevation, it fell back into the broad marble basin, and, as the filmy threads of water glittered in the moonlight, it looked like the silvery plumage of some giant helmet. And sweet and most soothing, too, was the low monotonous chant of the falling waters in the silent night, as they met the still waters of the pool beneath. One could fancy it the gentle, joyous greeting with which fair spirits, that have left heaven to wander awhile upon earth, throw themselves again into the bosoms of their sister spirits, when their wandering is over. Perhaps these sweet sounds did unconsciously break in upon the reverie of the old man, for he looked up for a moment and opened the fold of his gown, as it were to let the grateful freshness of the vapour to his bosom. But it was not for sights like these, beautiful though they were, that the old man was abroad to-night. Onward he hurried by the Sacred Way, passing through the Arches of Titus and Fabius, and between the Roman Forum and the Forum of Cæsar. Heeding not the wondrous congregation of arches, temples, and graceful columns that shot upwards into the heavens, the old man pressed forward still, till passing near the Arch of Septimius Severus, and the Temple of Concord, he stopped at the base of a strongly built and gloomy edifice, that even then bore the marks of great antiquity. This was the Mamertine prison. Ascending a flight of stone steps, cut through the hill, that led to an entrance on the second story, the person whose course we have been tracing stepped softly up to a door of solid oak, studded with huge rivets of iron, and smote the wood gently with his hand, repeating the act twice, at intervals. After the third signal, a voice from within asked—

"Who cometh hither?" To which he outside replied:—

"Peace be with thee."

Then the door was cautiously opened, just sufficiently to allow a man to pass through, and was again as cautiously closed when the old man had entered.

CHAPTER II.

AT the time we write of, the ancient prison of the Mamertine, which Ancus Martius had built in what was once the centre of the city, was still made use of for the reception of criminals charged with more than ordinary guilt; and amongst these were many Christian converts, as the "Acts of the Martyrs," in which it is frequently mentioned, abundantly testify. The upper story of this dismal prison had now its tenant, and towards it two persons were directing their steps. One was a young girl just entering upon womanhood; the other an old man—he whom we have been following through the silent streets of Rome. The girl held in her hand a small lamp, and was evidently the guide to the gloomy passage they were traversing. Her step was firm and unhesitating, and she carried the light apparently rather to guide the feet of her companion who followed her than her own, for she held it above her head, and rather behind her, so that its rays fell just before his face, leaving hers in darkness, while the old man, even with the aid of the light, stepped unsteadily and doubtfully. At length they reached the strong oaken door of the dungeon, and paused for a moment, for the voice of one from within was audible. He was sustaining his spirit with the memory of familiar and beloved words, and the old man, as he caught them, joined with moving lips, which gave no outward sound.

"Out of the depths have I cried unto the Lord.

"Lord, hear my voice; let thine ears be attentive to the voice of my supplications.

"I wait for the Lord; my soul doth wait, and in his word do I hope.

"My soul waiteth for the Lord more than they that watch for the morning."

There was a pause of a moment, and then the sounds were resumed:—

"Why art thou so heavy, O my soul? and why art thou so disquieted within me? Oh, put thy trust in God, for I will yet give him thanks, which is the help of my countenance and my God."

The voice of the prisoner ceased, and the girl, committing the lamp to her companion, drew forth from her girdle a large key and unlocked the door; then, withdrawing the bolts, they entered the chamber. The faint rays of the lamp, struggling through the gloom of the prison, showed the form of a man seated on a straw pallet, and fettered, both hands and feet. At first he moved not; but the voice of his visitor quickly aroused him.

"Valentinus," said the old man to the prisoner, in solemn and gentle accents—"Valentinus, my brother, the peace of the Lord be with thee."

The prisoner sprang upon his feet, the chains clanking upon his limbs as he moved forward.

"Callistus, beloved friend and master! is it indeed thyself? God, then, has blessed my efforts, and thou art safe. But tell me quickly, who has escaped beside thee?"

Callistus turned hesitatingly towards the young girl, but replied not. Valentine understood the meaning of the movement.

"Brother, thou mayest speak freely before this dear child; a light is even now arising to her out of darkness. Look at her and doubt not."

Callistus now, for the first time, bent a scrutinizing look upon the maiden. She stood retiringly near the door, as if ready to depart, yet loth to do so undismissed. Her arms were crossed upon her bosom with an air as meek as it was gentle. Her head was slightly inclined forward, and her thick black hair fell in long showers to her shoulders, displaying, as it parted in front, a face thin, pale, and pensive, though not unhappy; but the fixed expression of her open eyes, and the countenance slightly upturned, told the poor girl's doom—she was blind.

"Thou mayest indeed speak all thy mind before our good child Nerea. She knows all that has befallen me, and by her aid it is that I have been able to communicate with thee."

"If this be so," said Callistus, "I will speak freely. Know, dear Valentinus, that the timely intelligence thou gavest to thy friends has saved them. When Calpurnius, the prefect, sought them beyond the Esquiline Gate, he found none. Alas! I fear thou didst purchase their safety with thy own peril."

"It is even so," said the other, "but I repent it not. Calpurnius and his guard came upon me in the burial ground of the people. My intercourse with the Christians was proved, and I answered not falsely the questions of one in power, nor denied the name of Christ, and so I was haled hither, for what doom I know not."

"Alas! alas! we are at our wits' end, and in great peril; our souls are always in our hands. But say, how dost thou fare, in this sad dungeon, my Valentinus?"

"God hath raised up friends to me even here, and when I had almost said the darkness should cover me, then indeed was my night turned into day. My sufferings, and it may be my patience, have found favour with the keeper of my prison, Asterius, the chief officer of the prefect. He has eased my chains, though he cannot unloose them, and supplied my bodily wants, though he may not remove me from this gloomy dungeon. But, above all, my dear Callistus, it hath pleased our Great Master to give this poor lamb to me, to lead her into the fold; her ears have greedily drunk in the divine truth, and God hath given her a soul of light within her darkened body. Is it not so, dear Nerea? Tell the good Bishop Callistus, my child."

The girl moved reverently forward as she heard the holy title of the stranger, and sinking down on her knees, at the spot whence she heard his voice, said very gently, yet fervently :—

"It is indeed so. Venerable father, and thou, my dear teacher, pray for me."

"She is a catechumen," said Valentine, "and earnestly desires fuller admission into the Church. I will answer for her; and at a fitting time I would that she receive the rite of baptism at thy hands. Meantime, I beseech thee to perform that ceremony which our Church designs should teach catechumens to confess their sins, and to review their consciences."

Deeply moved, Callistus said, "Be it even so, brother."

Then he stooped down, and taking up a portion of the damp clay, he touched her eyes with it, and laying his hands solemnly upon the head of the still kneeling girl, said:—

"The Lord enlighten thee, my daughter! And now leave us for a season. We have that to speak of which must be discussed in private, and thou, too, shouldst retire, and meditate in secret upon the ceremony which has admitted thee into the higher state of catechumens."

Then the girl rose from her knees and departed.

Long and earnest converse did the two Christian men hold during that lonely night. The prospects of the persecuted Church of Christ occupied the hearts of these faithful and courageous men, and the imminent peril of the one, and the uncertain and scarce less perilous state of the other, were well-nigh forgotten in their deeper anxiety for the welfare of the dispersed and afflicted band amongst which they had both so recently communed and worshipped. The hours passed sadly and silently by whilst they were thus occupied. At length Nerea's low knock was heard at the door, and she came in and warned them of the danger to which Callistus's long tarrying would expose them. And so the venerable bishop arose and embraced Valentinus, then blessing them both, he resigned himself once more to the guidance of the sightless girl, and left the dungeon. The moon had long set, and the grey cold light of morning was dawning along the summit of the Esquiline Hill, when Callistus made his way towards the country through the Suburra and the gardens of Mæcenas.

CHAPTER III.

THE sun had set cloudlessly on the day succeeding the night in which Callistus and Valentinus held their conference. As his last rays fell upon the city, ere he sank beneath the Janiculum, they lit up the winding course of the yellow Tiber, the mausoleum and circus of Adrian, and the imperial gardens lying at the foot of the Vatican Hill; then, leaving these in twilight, the golden flush spread along the horizon, touching the lofty ridge of western hills along their summits, and throwing out against the clear sky the grey ruins of the Arx Janiculensis, the most ancient fortress of Rome, built by Ancus Martius, to protect the river from the depredations of Etruscan pirates. Night quickly followed upon the still short twilight, and the light, scant and dim even at noon, which struggled into the dungeon of the Mamertine through the single small opening high up near the roof, had become fainter and fainter to the eye of the solitary watcher, till at length it vanished altogether, leaving him in utter darkness. He was not, however, left much longer to his solitary meditations. The bars of his prison door were shot back, then it was softly opened, and Nerea's lamp again illuminated his darkness. The girl bore in one hand a lamp, in the other a basket containing a small flask of wine, some fruit, and a loaf of fine bread, and moving with unerring foot to the low stool which stood by the wall, she placed them upon it.

"Dear master," said she, turning her face in the direction where the clank of the fetters told her Valentine was sitting, "pardon me that I am somewhat late this evening. I tarried not willingly, but of constraint; but now I bring you somewhat to refresh you. Ah! that I dared do more for your comfort."

"My ever kind and good child, thou hast procured me all that is needful; what my great Master and His blessed Apostles often wanted. Truly God has sent thee to minister strength to my body, as His holy angels are ever about me to sustain my soul when it faints and is distrustful. God will surely bless thee, who ministerest thus even to the most unworthy of His servants!"

The maiden took the hand which the priest had laid kindly upon her head, and carrying it to her lips, kissed it with reverent gentleness ere she released it. After a moment she put her hand into the folds of her vesture, and drawing forth a few flowers, she said:—

"Dear father, I have brought you the earliest violets of Rome. I plucked them this morning on a bank beyond the Tiber; their fragrance caught my senses as I wandered in the fresh morning air, after I left thee last."

The priest took the flowers, and rubbed them in his hands; then inhaling their odour, said:—

"Now, dear Nerea, are they not doubly sweet? As the broken spirit is the sacrifice that God best loveth, so is the odour of the crushed flowers sweetest to the sense. Our Heathen wise men exhort us to be patient in tribulation; but the wisdom that cometh from above teacheth us to rejoice in it. Is not this a gracious revelation that shows us how to extract joy from sorrow, as our old fable tells of one who turned everything he touched into gold?"

"I know already," said the girl solemnly and

sadly, "that sorrow and privation teach us patience. When I wander with any of my companions in the gardens beyond the Tiber, and hear their joyous exclamations at the beautiful hues of flowers, the green of the fields, and the golden light of the sun, I understand them not, save that those hues must be sweet as the scent of flowers and herbs, and the light of the sun like the song of birds. Ah! well do I remember when with a young playmate I first sat by the side of a fountain, and she laughed out gleefully, and cried, 'See, see, Nerea; oh, beautiful! there are thou and I in the fountain, dancing and glittering like Naiades.' Then said I:—

"'Nay, thou art mocking me, Glycera. We are both here together on the bank, and yet thou sayest we are in the water. It cannot be, silly one.'

"But she persisted and said—'It is even as I say, Nerea.'

"Then was I angry; and I thrust my hand into the fountain, and I found nought but the fleeting waters, that moved to my touch; and I said, 'Now know I of a surety that thou deceivest me.' But others of our playmates came up, and Glycera asked them was it not so; and they said, indeed it was. But one whispered softly, yet not so softly as to escape my ear, 'Hush, Glycera, thou dost forget Nerea is blind.' Then I felt what it was to be blind; and I wept sore that night when alone in my chamber. By degrees I grew tranquil: and I sported again with my companions, and learned to believe that the world had many lovely things which I could never know, and to bear my fate with patience. Ah! will the time come, dear teacher, when shall I learn to rejoice in my afflictions, as thou sayest a Christian ought?"

"Even so, my Nerea, will it yet be, I trust, that thou shalt say, 'It is good for me that I have been afflicted.' I have prayed for thee without ceasing, through the watches of the night, my daughter; and it may be that I shall find favour with the Lord, and that thou shalt taste and see how gracious God is. But thou must have faith, and I, too—I to work, and thou to believe in the name of Him through whom I work."

The priest arose, and stood for some moments buried in profound contemplation. At length he said:—

"And now, daughter, leave me for a season: I would be alone; and take thou again with thee the fruit and wine, for this kind goeth not out by prayer and fasting. When it is midnight, come to me again."

The girl did as Valentine desired her, and, passing from the prison, he was again left alone.

How the priest was occupied during the hours that intervened, we may not say, for none have recorded it. That he spent the time in earnest prayer and holy meditation, it may be well believed, for when Nerea again sought the cell at midnight, she found Valentine on his knees beside his couch of straw, absorbed and motionless. Neither the drawing of the bolts, nor the grating of the door had touched his senses, or roused him from his ecstatic reverie. When at length he arose from his kneeling posture, the face of the priest shone with a heavenly lustre of one who had been in communion with his great spiritual Master. Then he took from his bosom a parchment roll, wherein were recorded, by the Holy Evangelists, the things which Jesus had done when on earth. And he sat down on his pallet, and the girl on the low stool before him, and he read to her how Christ had opened the eyes of the blind Bartimeus, and had given sight to the man who was blind from his birth, and whom He sent to wash in the pool of Siloam. And the saint discoursed long and ardently to the listening girl, opening the mysteries of the wondrous faith for which he had forsaken all the earth holds dear, and was even then willingly in bonds and imprisonment. Hours passed thus in exhortation, mingled with prayer and words of comfort. And now Valentine paused, and once again his spirit was wrapt in divine communion. Then he arose and stood up, and the girl knelt down, and he cried :—

"Oh Lord my God, let this child receive her bodily sight, as thou hast shed thy light upon her spirit."

The dim lamp shed its flickering rays upon the upturned face of the maiden, as she fixed her sightless orbs, suffused with tears, on the saint. Then he touched her eyes and said :—

"According to thy faith be it unto thee."

A shudder past over the pallid features of the excited and awe-touched girl, when lo! the light of the lamp sank in the exhausted vessel, and they were left in darkness.

CHAPTER IV.

It was about the hour of noon, on the day following the events we have last recorded. The sun that looked down on the Forum Romanum beheld a sight of surpassing splendour and architectural magnificence. Temples reared their beautiful porticos of white marble on every side—triumphal arches spanned the ways, and graceful columns shot up into heaven. Halls where justice was dispensed, and ambassadors met to discuss treaties—spots where the people assembled, and rostra whence orators addressed them —all were there still. Beneath the porticos that ran round this wondrous mart, were the shops of tradesmen and goldsmiths, and money-changers. While on the hills that rose above it, on either side, were the imperial residences of the Cæsars, and the citadel and temple of Jupiter Capitolinus. Where now are all these? Some still stand, weather-stained and defiled, doing battle bravely against time and fate, the flame and the earthquake. Some show a ruined shaft or tottering pediment, and others have perished utterly, and antiquarians and historians delve and plod through the desolate rubbish, and quarrel about the site of things that once filled the eyes and ears of mankind.

But to-day the Forum Romanum was thronged, as usual, with crowds of inhabitants, some hurrying to and fro on their various avocations, some entering the different temples, some pacing the arched porticos. Here were groups of merchants, there knots of idlers retailing the news of the day, discussing the merits of a popular orator, or criticizing the newest play or poem, while in another place might be seen vendors of goods displaying their wares. Upon the steps of the Comitium, half a dozen persons were collected in earnest conversation, and their number was constantly augmented by loiterers, who were attracted to the spot by the gesticulations of the speakers. A spruce little barber was engaged in an animated discussion with a burly soldier, while the crowd gathered around them, listening with wondering attention.

"I tell thee, Thraso," said the little man, "it is no fable, but as true as that I am Fabius, the barber of the Suburra. I had it from one whom I shaved this morning, and who had it from Drusus, the slave of Asterius."

"Thou hast too many vouchers for thy story, good Fabius," said the soldier. "Hadst thou seen it with thine own eyes, instead of through the tongues of so many, I might make shift to believe thee. *Credat Judæus*, say I."

"Hear him now, my masters," said the little barber, appealing to the bystanders. "Those men of war are no better than infidels. They will scarce believe in Jupiter, unless they see him brandishing his thunderbolt."

"What is this marvellous news, good tonsor?" said one who had just come up to the group. "I am but newly come from the country, and would fain learn what is stirring."

"Worshipful Lysippus," replied the barber with an obeisance, "thou shalt hear it on the instant, and judge if I have not good warrant for what I relate. By Castor and Pollux," he continued, eyeing the soldier askance in the confidence of being under the protection of one of his best customers, "he is no true man who doubts the word of an honest citizen."

A shout of laughter from the crowd followed the sally of the valiant barber, while one of his neighbours slapped him on the back, crying:—

"Well said, brave Fabius. *Habet.* Thou hast given the soldier a home-thrust. By Bacchus, I will stand a flask of Sicilian wine that thou hast the best of it. The shears against the sword any day."

"Peace, friends," said Lysippus, "and let us hear the story."

"Well, then," said the barber, "you must know that as I shaved a certain personage this morning, an honourable gentleman, and a notary of fair report as any in the city, he asked me, as usual, what was the news, whereupon I replied I had not as yet had any, for it was early. Nay, then, said he, thou hast not heard——"

"Oh, Venus! have done with thy babbling. To the point, friend, in the name of Jupiter."

"Well, then, in brief, the notary told me that Drusus told him that the daughter of Asterius—thou knowest poor Nerea—the blind girl, had got her sight by the favour of I know not which of the gods, and can now see as well as you or I."

"Papæ!" cried Lysippus, "a marvel truly. Why the maid was blind from her birth. Good Fabius, I fear the notary has been putting a jest upon thee. Away, man, and mind thy stall, or thou mayest get into the hands of the prefect, and scarce come off with a dose of hellebore."

"Who is right now, my masters?" said Thraso, exultingly. "Come, Simo, and pay me that flask of Sicilian: thou hast lost it fairly."

The laugh was now turned relentlessly against the little tonsor. He slunk away discomfited and grumbling; the group dispersed, and each one joined some other party, to loiter or to labour, as their tastes or duties dictated.

But the tale of the barber fell not altogether upon unfruitful soil. There are few stories that will not gain credence with some one. By degrees, the rumour spread through other channels, and gained confirmation from quarters more faithworthy than a loquacious barber of the Suburra: and ere the sun had set, the wonderful tale was noised about throughout Rome, as a fact beyond all controversy, and a matter that had been brought under the prefect's notice.

And indeed there was good foundation for these reports. The situation which Asterius held, as the chief officer of Calpurnius, the prefect of the city, made concealment, if it were sought for, a matter not easily to be accomplished. But in truth, such did not seem to be the object of him or his family. The father loved his child tenderly, for she was an only one and motherless, and that tenderness was infinitely augmented by the poor girl's calamity. Her blindness, while it made her an object of solicitude and dependence to her parent, increased his love by keeping her constantly in his thoughts and much in his presence, and the devotion with which she returned his care, added to the gentle and almost cheerful patience with which she endured her privation, served to draw more closely around the heart of the father those bonds of affection which nature had originally tied with no weak hand. Nerea, as she grew up, was able, in some sort, to repay the kindness of her parent. She had learned to traverse the Mamertine prison, and to aid her father in his custody. She knew each cell, and could reach it with speed and certainty in the hours of darkness, and though her nature was sensitive, yet was it kind and compassionate, and so she took a deep interest, if not a pleasure, in visiting the cells, and supplying comforts to its inmates, as far as the prison discipline would allow. Nerea was, therefore, well known in her own locality; and when at early morning, or eventide, she passed towards the Palatine Bridge, on her way to the gardens on the further side of the Tiber, or even, on rare occasions, ventured to thread her way across the Forum, there was always sure to be a ready hand to remove from her path any casual obstruction. Many a commiserating and respectful look was turned on her, and many a kind greeting was offered to the blind girl of the Mamertine.

When Valentine was thrown into the Mamertine prison, which was some weeks previous to the visit of Callistus, Nerea's occupation brought her acquainted with him. His resignation under his trial quickly interested the girl in no ordinary degree. Her kind and compassionate attention to him excited on his part a corresponding interest in her. And the Christian found, unexpectedly, that Providence had afforded him, even in his dungeon, an opportunity of preaching the faith for which he was then in bonds, that occupied his mind and alleviated his sorrow. By degrees he opened to her the sublime truths of his religion, and in his auditress he found a willing disciple. The infirmity of the poor girl, while it shut her out, in a great measure, from the contemplation of sensible objects, left her mind free for the reception of the things that lie beyond and above the senses. And so, from day to day, she listened to the disclosure of the unseen realities of spiritual life, and her soul meditated upon them in the hours of that bodily darkness which was ever present to her. Thus it was that when, by her assistance, a sure message was conveyed to the Christian band which was then suffering from the recently revived persecution in Rome, and that Callistus visited the cell of Valentine, she had so far advanced in the knowledge and belief of the true faith as to be accounted fit for the ceremony of imposition of hands and anointing of the eyes, which the bishop, on the assurance of her catechist, had administered.

Who shall describe the sensations of awe and amazement, of delight and holy thankfulness which agitated the soul of the once blind maiden, when the light of day, beaming upon her eyes, disclosed to them the innumerable wonders of the fair world around her? Who shall tell the joy of her father's heart at the marvellous and to him scarce credible event? Weeping upon the bosom of her parent all was told. Asterius hastened to the cell, and poured forth his gratitude in disordered words. And Valentine lost not the opportunity which the occasion offered. In profound and humble adoration, the saint first poured out his heart before the Father of light and life, and then directed the agitated heart of his keeper to the knowledge of Him by whose power the miracle was wrought. And then the young maid silently joined them, and the three remained together for many hours, the priest teaching, the parent and child listening. So the work of conversion went on, and two more souls were added to the Church of Christ.

Meantime the strange event was noised abroad, first in vague and conflicting rumours, and then more circumstantially, till at length the fame of it reached the ears of the prefect of the city. The jurisdiction of that officer was, at the time we write of, most comprehensive, embracing not only matters of police, but almost every civil and criminal case. Duty cast upon him the investigation of the report. A rigid inquiry followed, which resulted in the establishing of the fact, and the manner in which it had taken place. It was too momentous, both as regarded the religion of the State and the position of the Christians, to be dealt with by the prefect, and, in the absence of the Emperor Claudius (then in Pannonia), the magistrate referred without delay to the Senate an occurrence which he deemed involving the crime of sorcery. Asterius and Nerea were summoned to the presence of that august tribunal. Proof of the fact was easy, for many were there who could attest that she who tranquilly, almost fearlessly, raised her mild intelligent eyes to look on her judges was indeed the blind daughter of the keeper of the Mamertine. But proof was needed not: father and daughter avowed the fact, and declared that they, too, were Christians. The double crime of being disciples of the false religion, and implicated in practices of forbidden arts and sorcery, was established against Valentine, Asterius, and Nerea. The former was condemned to death, and the two latter were removed, and cast fettered into the prison where they had so often tended others, and ministered to the comforts of the suffering.

CHAPTER V.

MORNING dawned upon the Imperial City, and the rays of the sun shone down upon the palaces of the

Cæsars, the domes of temples, and the summits of triumphal arches and lofty columns. It was the 16th day of the kalends of March, being, according to our computation of time, the 14th of February.

As the rays of day penetrated through the opening high up in the wall of one of the cells in the Mamertine prison, it diffused through the dungeon a dim and partial twilight, which fell upon the figures of four persons. With three of these we are already familiar. Valentine lay in profound meditation on his pallet, and near him were seated, also in bonds, Asterius and Nerea; the fourth wore the garb of a soldier of the prefect's guard,—the watch who had been set on the prisoners during the night; but, as he turned his face, the light fell upon its features and revealed those of Callistus. Through the agency of some friends of Asterius, the bishop had contrived to assume the dress and take the place of the soldier whose duty it was during that night to keep watch upon the prisoners within the cell, and thus was he enabled to minister comfort and spiritual consolation to them during this season of sore trial, and for the last time to partake of the sacred elements with Valentine. And now Callistus advanced towards Valentine, and touching him with his hand, said:—

"Brother, I may not tarry much longer; the light

of morning is growing strong, and the watch will soon come to relieve me."

Valentine arose, and answered:—

"It is, indeed, even as thou sayest, and my time draws nigh. I am now ready to be offered up. Shall I not rejoice that I am accounted worthy to suffer, even as did our beloved Paul himself, who lay in chains and darkness in this very dungeon where we now are?"

"Is there, then, no hope of escape?" said Asterius. "Hast thou conveyed my message and the ring to him whom I mentioned, O Callistus?"

"I have so done," replied the bishop; "but hope of aid in that quarter is vain,—the Senate may not be interfered with on this point."

"Yet there is one other chance of life left for Valentine. Say thou wilt permit it? Ah, will not I and mine joyfully peril life and limb for him who has given me and my Nerea light and life?"

The bishop shook his head dissentingly; but Valentine arose, and said almost sternly:—

"Is this, then, Asterius, the fruit that thou bearest of my teaching? Wouldst thou violate the law, and oppose thyself to the powers that are set over us? Surely I have shown thee that they are ordained of God, and that obedience to them in all things that God permits them to enforce, is the Christian's duty. Grieve my spirit no more with such thoughts, but let the few moments that remain for us to pass together be employed to a better purpose. Father," he continued, turning towards Callistus, "what hinders that these should be baptized? I have already instructed them thereunto, and I would the more joyfully leave this earthly tabernacle knowing that these my children in the Lord had received the gift and grace, and that, in the day when He maketh up his jewels, they too may be His."

"I will do thy desire in this matter, dear brother," answered the bishop. "I may the more safely dispense with the longer probation which the Church in ordinary cases wisely directs, seeing that the hand of God has visibly worked in their case, and also that they are themselves in peril of their lives, and a more convenient opportunity may never arise."

Saying this, the good bishop took the vase of water which stood beside the pallet, and pouring forth some of it into the drinking cup, prepared himself for the solemn rite. Meantime, Asterius and Nerea, having been previously instructed by Valentine as to their deportment and duty, stood forward before the bishop, turning their faces towards the west, and stretching out their fettered hands, each in turn said:—

"*I renounce Satan and his works, and his pomps, and his service, and his angels, and his inventions, and all things that belong to him or are subject to him.*"

Then they struck their hands together, to denote more emphatically by gesture their abhorrence of their great spiritual adversary. After this renunciation came the vow or covenant of obedience to their new Master. As in the former ceremony, the early Christians turned towards the west as the region of darkness, whose power they renounced, so in this they changed their position, facing the east,—the region of light, the place of the rising sun, which was the type of the Sun of Righteousness whom they now sought, and by this change symbolizing their turning from darkness to light—from Satan to Christ. Thus turning, and with hands and eyes lifted up to Heaven, the parent and child made their profession in the appointed words:—

"*I give myself up to thee, O Christ, to be governed by thy laws.*"

Then Callistus put to them several questions with regard to their belief in the summary of faith contained in the creed, which when they had answered, he took the water, and making over it the sign of the cross, consecrated it by the prayer used in the liturgy of the ancient Church. After this he divested them of their garments, so far as their bonds would permit, and performed the rite of baptism by aspersion, or sprinkling, which was, on extraordinary occasions, then allowed to be substituted for the more general practice of immersion, and signing their foreheads thrice with the sign of the cross in the name of the Persons of the Trinity, he admitted them into the visible Church of Christ.

The sacrament was scarce administered when the measured tread of feet without the door warned those in the prison that the time for relieving the watch had arrived. Callistus, lifting up his hands, bestowed on the three the benediction which was given to the Christians:—

"*The Lord bless thee and keep thee; The Lord lift up the light of his countenance upon thee and bless thee.*"

Then he flung himself upon the neck of Valentine, and cried, "Alas! my brother, the Lord support thee." And Valentine replied:—

"Surely, I know He will; but weep not for me, for I feel to die is gain."

Upon this the clank of the opening door was heard, and Callistus said softly:—

"The Lord keep thee in all thy ways. Assuredly I will be near thee at the last."

Then placing on his head the helmet, and concealing his person in the folds of his robe, he advanced to the entrance of the prison, and passed forth.

CHAPTER VI.

THE dawn of morning had brightened into broad daylight, Rome had shaken off her night-sleep, and life was again astir in her. By degrees the busy crowds were again pouring into the streets; the forums began to fill with occupants; the waggons were entering the city from the country, and the bustle of daily traffic was once more resumed. Groups of persons began insensibly to congregate about the Arch of Septimius Severus, and the Temples of Concord, of Fortune, and of Jupiter Tonans. Others might be seen ranged in tiers along the steps that wound round the Mamertine prison from the eastern angle of it, and ominously named the *Scalæ Gemoniæ*, from the groans of those who thus ascended to the dungeons; while more began to perch themselves between the pillars which formed the long colonnade of the Tabularium, whence they looked down upon the scene below. It was manifest, from the expectant looks of the people, and the disposition to take up their position on the highest steps they could attain, that some spectacle had drawn them together. Every favourable spot for observation was now occupied by dense masses of people, when a little man forced his way hurriedly up the flight of steps leading to the portico of the temple of Concord. Touching the foot of a man who stood above him, the new-arrived addressed him in a breathless tone:—

"I beseech thee, by all the gods, dear Simo, give me thine hand that I may climb up beside thee."

"Impossible, Fabius," said he who was thus earnestly entreated. "Were I to stoop down to aid thee, I would lose my balance and fall from my place; besides, there is not room here for a lizard."

"Nay, but indeed thou must not desert me in this strait, Simo. I will not take much space, thou knowest; and I promise thee we shall have a cup of wine together when all is over. I will repay thee that thou lost to Thraso the other day, and with usury." This last argument was not without effect. Simo made shift to give the barber his hand, and with some difficulty and disturbance of his neighbours at both sides, who did not fail to vent their annoyance in that choice phraseology in which the Roman populace were adepts, the little man was hoisted up by the side of his friend.

"How happens it, Fabius, that thou art so late to-day? It is not thy wont to be the last where aught is to be seen or heard."

"Thou sayest true, Simo. I was just stepping out of my shop, a good half hour since, when one who would not be denied entered, and sitting down, forced me to shave his beard. But hast seen aught yet?"

"Nothing: but tell me, what knowest thou of this matter?"

"What know I? Much, my masters,"—for the little barber always made it a point to address himself to every one within hearing. "This Valentinus is one of the most obstinate of this Jewish sect, and, like his creed, bears no loyalty to Cæsar, or love to the gods. Not only did he refuse to do sacrifice to the gods, but he blasphemed and contemned them, and averred there was no God but he who raised the insurrection in Judea at the time of our Emperor Tiberius."

"They are truly an arrogant sect, and disturbers of public tranquillity withal," said one of the group.

"Ay," responded another, "'tis a malignant superstition; they hate mankind, and practise in secret loathsome rites. I have heard that they partake of Thyestean feasts, devouring young children and drinking their blood."

"But you have not yet heard the strangest piece of this fellow's audacity," resumed the barber. "You all know, doubtless, how that it pleased the gods to give sight to the blind girl Nerea, when she was lately praying in the Temple of the goddess Fortuna hard by. Well, this Valentinus, hearing of the miracle, gives out that it was he wrought it through the power of his God. And he had so bewitched the girl with his spells and potions, that she would not gainsay him, though it is alleged there were many witnesses present in the Temple when she was cured."

"Hush," cried Simo, "here comes the prefect's guard; they will pass near us presently."

As he spoke the eyes of all were turned in the direction in which he pointed. A strong guard of soldiers was seen moving from the base of the steps leading to the Mamertine prison. Presently they came opposite the spot where Fabius and his auditors were collected. In the midst of the company of soldiers walked one on whom all eyes were fixed— a man about the prime of life, and of the middle stature. His bared head was erect, and the brown hair fell adown it in light curls. His full blue eyes were turned slightly towards heaven, as in contemplation of things beyond the earth. Full of sweetness and love was his whole countenance, and there played around it a soft and almost radiant expression, which resembled less a smile than the influence of some rapturous feeling. Firmly and calmly he walked along; and when the shouts and revilings of the brutal populace from time to time assailed him, he looked up at his persecutors with unperturbed eyes, that had more of pity than anger in their placid survey. Such was Valentine, the Christian priest, who, by the sentence of the Senate, was now led forth to his execution. The band of soldiers, with their prisoner, moved slowly onwards through the crowds that pressed upon them on every side, and, winding along the base of the Capitoline Hill, they passed the forums of Augustus and Trajan, and through the ancient wall of the city, built by Servius Tullius, into the Flaminian Way. The populace in the forums, as soon as the party had passed, rushed forward, by various ways, through the Campus Martius, to gain the Flaminian Gate, and the whole of that long road which now forms the magnificent street of the Corso was lined with a dense mass of human beings as Valentine and his guards passed along. At length they reached the gate in the walls of Honorius and Valerian, which then formed the northern boundary of the city, and passed into the open space beyond it. Here was the spot upon which preparation had been made for carrying into execution the sentence against the Christian. Being placed in the midst, the prefect of the city came forward, and, for the last time, put to him the question which was to decide his fate,—for it was the established custom, even at the last moment, to remit the sentence, if the condemned renounced his faith and sacrificed to the gods.

"Valentinus, art thou a Christian?"

And Valentine said:—

"I am."

Then the prefect again addressed him, and said:—

"Wilt thou renounce Christ, and swear by the name of Cæsar?—wilt thou do sacrifice to the gods?"

Whereupon Valentine replied:—

"Thy gods are the work of men's hands, and thy religion the device of their corrupt hearts. There is no god but the God whom Christians serve."

At a sign from the prefect two men came forward, and they stripped Valentine of his outward robe, so that he stood in his tunic. At this moment an old soldier from behind touched him, and said softly:—

"Courage, Valentine. Be strong in the Lord."

The face of the priest beamed with joyful alacrity as he recognised the voice of Callistus.

"Dominus illuminatio mea," cried he, looking up. "The Lord is my light in this hour of my trial with the powers of darkness. God is our refuge and strength,—a very present help. In him have I put my trust; I will not be afraid what man can do unto me."

The soldiers were then proceeding to tie a bandage around his eyes; but Valentine said gently:—

"Suffer me to depart with unmuffled sight. I would willingly look my last upon the heavens."

The men, apparently moved by his entreaty, looked towards the prefect, who suffered his request to be granted, being contented that his hands should be bound. While this was doing, the Christian priest seemed to lose sight of the things around him, and to be absorbed wholly in spiritual contemplation. His eyes were intently fixed on the bright sky, to the eastward, and his lips moved with words which the multitude understood not. But one there was, nigh at hand, who knew them, and rejoiced in the midst of the trial of his brother, as he heard these ejaculations:—

"Who shall separate us from the love of Christ? Shall tribulation, or distress, or persecution, or famine, or nakedness, or peril, or sword?"

"In all these things we are more than conquerors, through Him that loved us.

"Neither death nor life, nor angels, nor principalities, nor powers, nor things present, nor things to come, shall be able to separate us from the love of God, which is in Christ Jesus our Lord."

Callistus bowed his head in resignation and hope.

"Father," sighed he, "not our will, but thine be done."

A swaying of the multitude, and a shout, caused him to look up; and the headless and bleeding trunk of the martyr, Valentine, lay before him!

"The blood of the martyrs is the seed of the Church." The blood of God's saints was not shed in vain on the soil of pagan Rome. Scarce a century elapsed before a Church, bearing his name, stood on the spot where Valentine had suffered; and in later time, another was erected to his memory, near the Ponte Molo; and when Christian emperors swayed the Roman sceptre, the Flaminian Way and Gate, through which the saint passed on his way to his martyrdom, were known as the Via and Porta Valentiniana.

The stranger who now visits Rome may wander over the scene of our story; yet how changed its aspect and fortunes! He can enter through the magnificent gate, the "Porta di Popolo," which the genius of Canina has constructed, and pass down through the palaces that line the Corso on either side. He may wander through her forums; but he will look in vain for the living grandeur of the imperial city—

> ———"tra l' erbe
> Cercando i grandi avanzi e le superbe
> Reliquie dello splendor latino."

Her temples are prostrate; her palaces unroofed and in ruins; her arches and columns defaced and broken. All so changed that the antiquarian pauses often in doubt, amidst the lonely and half-unburied ruins around, before he will venture to pronounce to what temple belong the still beautiful shafts that meet his eye, or fix the spot where the citizens met in their assembly, or the orators pleaded for their clients.

Yet over the pagan ruins and the pagan memories rise on every side the Christian shrines. Many a cross is now planted, and many a pilgrim prays in the area of that circus which drank the blood of Christ's saints, as it flowed in rivers on its stones. And if the memory of Valentine arise to the mind, as the visitor lingers near the Roman Forum let

THE MARTYR.

him turn his footsteps to the Church of San Pietro in Carcere, and he will be shown the Mamertine prison, with some of its steps still remaining; and the cell where Paul lay in chains, and Valentine made converts.

NOTE.—St. Valentine, whose festival day is the 14th February, is called a Bishop in some of the modern Calendars; but the ancient historians of the Church and all the Martyrologies which I have been able to consult call him simply "Presbyter." There was, no doubt, an African bishop of that name, but he who suffered martyrdom in Rome had not attained to that rank in the Church.

Easter Day.

ST. MARY'S-SUPER-MARE.

CHAPTER I.

LIFE AND DEATH.

Hamlet.—Has this fellow no feeling of his business? he sings at grave-making.

Horatio.—Custom has made it in him a property of easiness.

SHAKESPEARE.

IF I am to have the selection of the place of my last repose—which it is not at all likely that I shall—I know no spot of earth where I should more willingly lie down and stretch my bones at full length, than in the churchyard of St. Mary's-super-Mare. There is not a sweeter, sunnier nook in the south of England; a greener or a softer sod one may find nowhere; a calmer or more sequestered hiding-place, where the life-wearied soul may lay down his burden of humanity till the great day when he shall once more clothe himself in his mortal coil. Not, indeed, that I am very fastidious about such matters; though I confess to a weakness, if you will so call it. I would not wish to lie in a city burial-ground, huddled away into some close, smoky corner, intruding upon the former tenant of the spot, and in my turn to be disturbed and disarranged for the next visitant; committing posthumous offences against society, by adding to the poisonous miasma of the thronged and festering charnel-house.

'Twas a fine, bright, airy day in the end of March. The wind swept freshly over the dark, solemn yew trees in the churchyard, and whistled through the louvred windows of the church tower, shaping itself into wild, strange voices, that rose and fell fitfully upon the ear. Upon the western side of the churchyard, just where the shadows of the yew trees invaded the bright golden sunshine that fell upon the greensward—for the sun had now passed the meridian some hours, and was sinking in the heavens—a hale old man, in a smock frock, with thick-soled shoes, and old leathern leggings, was delving knee-deep in the soil. 'Twas the sexton at his customary occupation, digging a grave. From time to time he sang, in a low, pleasant voice, a snatch of an old ballad to cheer him at his toil; and, as he met now and then a bone, he tilted it up lightly on his mattock, and laid it aside, with that habitual care which a gardener would show in removing a stone from a flower-bed, but without any of that reverence which is generally felt for the remains of the dead. Two or three little children were sporting about, hiding behind the tomb-stones, and now and then showing their merry, chubby faces, glowing with health, above some white, cold slab, laughing out shrilly, and mocking and flouting, as it were, the chill, stern repose of death.

"Good afternoon, Robin," said a voice near the old man; "I have been looking for you down in the village, and the old dame told me I would find you here."

The sexton looked up, and saw a young farmer of the neighbourhood, who had been lately married.

"Ah! Master Gubbins, is that you? Good afternoon to you. And how is your pretty mistress, these times?"

"Faith, bravely, Robin. But I want a cast of your office."

The old fellow looked at the young one with a subdued humour, such as a sexton might be supposed not improperly to indulge in, as he asked,—

"What office, Master Gubbins? Nothing *this* way, I suppose?" and he cast up a mattock-full of fresh loam by way of illustration.

"Oh no, thankee; no, not just at present," answered the farmer, with a hearty laugh. "We shall have a few of the neighbours at the Grange this evening, and my *Missus* sent me to fetch you and the fiddle· she says there'll be no sport without you."

"Business first, Master Gubbins; business first, and pleasure after. This here job must be finished in an hour; the parson sent word that the funeral would be here by four o'clock.

"Whose funeral, goodman?" asked the farmer; "who is dead in these parts?"

"Oh, only the lady that came last month with her husband to lodge down at Dame Ashley's. Nobody knows anything about them but the young curate, for they never stirred out except of an evening to take a walk. The old dame says she was far gone in a decline when she came here, and the poor thing wasted away from day to day. They say the gentleman is a painter, or something of that sort, from London. Well, Master Gubbins, I'll be off to the Grange as soon as the funeral is over, and I have laid the last sod on this here grave. It won't be my fault, by no means, if you haven't a merry night on't."

The old fellow thereupon set to digging with redoubled energy, and the young man went his way. After a time old Robin rested on his mattock, and surveyed his work with the self-satisfied air of a man who is proud of his skill; then he gave an artistic touch or two along the margin to make it smooth and trim; and, wiping his face with the sleeve of his frock, he sat down on the edge of the grave, and drawing from his pocket a piece of bread and some cheese, he commenced to munch them leisurely. It was a strange subject for contemplation—that hard-featured old man sitting in the grave which he had just prepared for the young and lovely dead—sitting and eating, and then smoking his pipe, and sucking in his lean jaws as he inhaled the pleasant odour! Life and Death, as it were, meeting upon neutral ground, and suspending for a season their ancient, world-long feud, and looking each upon the other with undisturbed eye. And yet is it not well that it should be so? If every living man may say, as truly as did David to Jonathan, "there is but one step between me and death;"—if the darker phantom ever follows the brighter one, as closely as the shadow follows upon the sunlight; —if, in the words of one of our poets—words strangely prophetic of his own destiny—

> "Death is here, and death is there,
> Death is busy everywhere;
> All around—within, beneath,
> Above is death, and we are death!"—

is it not indeed well that man should learn to familiarise himself with the contemplation of a doom that is inevitable? It is God's ordinance, and Nature's prompting, that man shall cherish and love his life—that he shall do with diligence whatsoever his hand findeth to do, undismayed by any slavish fear of death. We may not indeed rob death of his power, though we may disarm him of his terrors; not by a brutish insensibility, but by a manly preparation. For my own part, I believe that the man who thinks most upon death is practically most energetic in the use of life. Above all, he will be so if he look upon the grave not only as the gate of death, but as the gate of life too. And so while, like old Robin, he may walk all day amongst tombs, he will do more; he will in thought stoop down and enter in, as did the disciples, and hear spiritual voices proclaiming that death holds no soul in thraldom—that the occupant of the grave "is not here, for he is risen."

I am not disposed to think that reflections such as these occupied the mind of the old sexton of St. Mary's-super-Mare. At all events, when he had finished his frugal meal, and smoked out his pipe, he went to work again right heartily, and ere long completed his task to his entire satisfaction.

CHAPTER II.

THE GATE OF DEATH.

> "Von dem Dome,
>   Schwer und bang,
>   Tönt die Glocke
>   Grabgesang,
>   Ernst begleiten ihre Trauerschläge
>   Einen Wandrer aut dem letzten Wege."
> SCHILLER.

THE sun had sunk more than half way down the heavens, and the old yew trees cast their shadows longer, and deeper, and more solemn, over the churchyard of St. Mary's-super-Mare. And now the clock chimed out the hour of four; and then from the tower the bell pealed forth at intervals its slow, monotonous, dirge-like notes—sounds which ever fall sadly on the ear, for they tell of the spirit that has passed away. In a few moments the gate of the churchyard was thrown open, and a funeral procession passed through it, and moved onwards towards the new-made grave. Few, indeed, were they who composed that little train; the half-dozen men who bore the palled coffin, and as many more to relieve them, with one or two of the shopkeepers from the village, and old Dame Ashley's son. Before the coffin walked the young curate of the parish, in his white surplice, reading at intervals those sublime and solemnizing sentences which proclaim Christ as the resurrection and the life, and announce that the dead shall rise in their flesh, and behold the Redeemer with their eyes. And close behind that shell—close, as if he were jealous that even the air of heaven should intervene between him and the all-beloved—walked, with bowed head and unsteady step, a young, slight, pale man, noticing nothing around him, absorbed in the silent grief that gave no outward sign.

And now the psalms are said, and the coffin is lowered down to its final resting-place, and the young curate has pronounced those versicles so deeply confessing man's misery and weakness; so full of wailing humiliation, of importunate prayer, that no one can hear them for the first time with an unmoistened eye, nor for the hundredth time with an unmoved heart. And the poor bereaved husband stood the while at the grave's edge, and hung over as if he too would have fallen into it; and he hid his face in his hands, that none might see his grief;

and when old Robin, fixing his eye on the curate, flung down, with all the precision of a practised hand, the clay upon the coffin—once—twice—thrice— the mourner shuddered sensibly, as if then, indeed, he felt that death had come in bodily form and ravished for ever from him the life of his life, thrusting a cold hand into his bosom and plucking 'forth his heart, leaving him to live henceforth as best he might without it.

How long he may have remained thus insensible to external objects, the young man knew not. At length a hand was laid gently upon his shoulder, and a low, kind, yet solemnly cheerful voice addressed him :—

"Come, my dear Mr. Travers, you must not sorrow as one that has no hope. Let me lead you hence, now; you must come with me to my quiet bachelor's fireside. If I may not minister to your consolation, I shall not at least disturb your sorrow. Come, my dear sir."

The young widower looked up. All had gone from the churchyard except themselves and old Robin, the sexton, who was methodically replacing the green sods upon the grave, already filled up. Travers mastered his emotion sufficiently to reply to the curate :—

"Sir, I thank you; but I cannot, indeed I cannot—at least not just now. I would be alone, if you please."

The curate knew enough of the human heart, and of the man beside him, to be sensible how vain a thing it is to reason down human sorrow in the first rush of its overflow; and he had seen enough of the sweet spirit, whose body lay beneath them, not to wonder at the intensity of the survivor's grief. So he pressed kindly his hand, and went his way in silence. Old Robin, meantime, worked away with the imperturbable steadiness of forty years' professional habit. He had witnessed such scenes as this oftener than he could number. Some people might grieve more, and some less; one might linger at the grave side longer than another; but then Robin did not take any note of these distinctions, and he ranged them all in the common category of "folks that take on for a while at first, and then ——" So, when he had laid down the last sod, and given it a final patting with the back of his mattock, he shouldered that implement, and took his departure to get his fiddle, and contribute to the pleasures of the evening at Farmer Gubbins's, of the Grange.

CHAPTER III.

THE SHADOW ON THE GRAVE.

"As the cloud is consumed and vanished away; so he that goeth down to the grave shall come up no more."—JOB, vii. 9.

LOWER and lower sunk the sun in the heavens; and deeper and deeper fell the shadows of the dark yew trees athwart the churchyard of St. Mary's-super-Mare, till they swallowed up in their gloom the new-made grave wherein the young dead had been so lately placed. One lay stretched along the cold, damp sod, motionless in all the abandonment of despair. At length, Frederick Travers arose slowly from the ground, and sat down upon a tombstone close by the grave of his beloved. Then passed in review before his mind the events of the last few months; yet dim in their colouring, and indistinct in their outlines, more like the visions of a distempered dream, or the figures which the shade of the phantasmagoria cast upon the screen at midnight, than the realities of life. There stood before him the fair young maiden, high-born and tenderly nurtured; she whom he had long loved in secret with a hopeless, yet irrepressible passion. Then came the sweet, yet tumultuous hour of the heart's revelations, when the head of the proud, rich man's daughter lay on the bosom of the poor painter, and the pure, meek, loving soul of the maiden confessed the power of genius and of worth. Another scene, and the tearful, trembling girl steals forth in the shadow of the evening, and the painter meets her, and leads her lovingly, yet reverently, as he would have guided a stainless angel out of heaven, till he places her beneath his matron sister's roof. Yet another scene, and the merry bells peal out in a far-away sylvan hamlet—the homestead of his happy boyhood; and now, a happier man, he leads the patrician's daughter to the altar steps, and she becomes the painter's bride. Ah! how bright are the colours that paint this scene upon his memory and his brain! how tender and warm the light that bathes and enwraps these two blissful creatures that pass along the field of imagination's vision! But, lo! the light fades, the shadows arise, and the scene changes. See that fair young matron again—oh! too fair now, for the roses on that sweet cheek are paling; the lustre in that pure, deep well of truthfulness—that meek, dove-like eye—is growing dim and troublous; for a father's curse has found her, and the breath of the malediction withers her beauty, and weighs down her soul! Then comes sickness of body with sorrow of heart;

the wasting form—the feeble limbs. And now they seek a milder region; and with trembling haste and troubled heart, her husband bears her southward. Then comes another change—fading, fading, day by day—the curse ever preying upon her gentle and remorseful soul. Yet does she cling with an undivided and undiminished love to him for whom she has given up so much in this world—for whom she has risked so much in the world to come. And he, the poor, stricken, maddened husband, how does he cling to hope, even where there is no room to hope! how does he watch, and tend, and crush down to calmness, for her sake, the agony of a bursting and rebellious heart! But in vain, all in vain: the gloom deepens, deepens into the darkness of night, as the last scene rises to view—the sick chamber, the heavy air—the closed curtains, the long, long, deep night of unuttered—unutterable sorrow and silent watching; the quick-drawn breathing, the fluttering pulse, the languid head, tossing restlessly in a vain effort for repose: then comes the wan, sickly, cold dawn of the morning, and then the dim eye lightens with a faint illumination of ineffable love; and the poor, thin, white hand faintly presses his own; and then—but he sees no more: the vision vanishes; the dream gives place to the horrible reality before him—a green fresh mound swelling up above the black earth that holds what was his all in the world. And where is she now? Can the grave answer him that awful question? What hope is there beyond the tomb? The black shadow of the yew trees hung like a heavy mantle over that grave, and the words of Job came across his soul as an answer to his question. "I go whence I shall not return; even to the land of darkness, and the shadow of death. A land of darkness, even as darkness itself and of the shadow of death, without any order, and where the light is darkness." With a bitter, despairing cry, he closed his eyes, and fell back upon the tombstone.

When Travers arose to consciousness from the stupor of his grief, the short twilight had faded away, and given place to night. The thin, pale crescent of the young moon was now glittering in a blue, tranquil sky, and myriads of stars were diffusing their tremulous light through the vault of heaven, and down upon the low-lying earth; but they brought no comfort to the soul of the mourner; his grief was yet too fresh and too strong to endure consolation. All things on earth spoke to him of gloom and sorrow; all in heaven of a majesty remote, sublime, serene, and inaccessible—untouched, as it were, with a feeling of man's infirmity or misfortune; too high for man's degradation; too holy for man's sinfulness. Yes, that moon and those stars spoke to him in language of awful reproof; their light fell upon his spirit but to make it all the darker. "How," they seemed to say, "can man be justified with God? or how can he be clean that is born of a woman? Behold even to the moon, and it shineth not; yea, the stars are not pure in his sight. How much less man, that is a worm; and the son of man, which is a worm."

With slow and tottering steps the young man passed forth from the dwellings of the dead. At the gate of the churchyard he turned once again to look at the grave of her whom he had loved so truly; but it was now undistinguishable in the gloom of night. A dreadful hopelessness chilled his heart. He felt as the father of his race may have felt when he turned his steps from Eden, and saw the sword of the cherubim intercept his return for ever. Aye, there stood Azrael with his sword, separating the living from the dead: the dead! oh, mystery of mysteries! where are they? what are they? "The living know that they shall die; but the dead know not anything, neither have they any more a reward, for the memory of them is forgotten. Also their love, and their hatred, and their envy is now perished; neither have they any more a portion for ever in anything that is done under the sun."

CHAPTER IV.

THE LIGHT FROM THE CROSS.

"To them which sat in the region and shadow of death light is sprung up."—MATT. iv. 16.

WHEN I see a church, especially in the country parts, rising in the midst of its peaceful graveyard, with the tombs and graves all around, I feel how strong is the instinct which leads man to seek support and protection from the Deity at that dread hour, when the soul takes her departure from the body upon an untried and unknown journey. However successfully we may withdraw ourselves from God during life, Death, his janitor, is sure to force us at last into his presence. And while the soul awaits her doom from God, men place the body within the precincts of some spot which its maker is supposed more particularly to sanctify; there to lie till the day when all flesh shall arise, and the soul shall reclothe herself in her garments of humanity.

The church of St. Mary's-super-Mare was one of those beautiful old structures which, in mediæval times, had arisen through our land: cruciform, with a tower rising from the intersection of the transept, whence sprang a tapering spire, surmounted by a gilded cross. The doorway was pointed gothic, and the eastern window caught the light upon the many-tinctured glass of its ornamented rose. All around lay the graves of the departed, like sheep gathering round the great shepherd; fearfully, yet confidingly sheltering, as it were, from the influences of the "prince of the power of the air," beneath the guardianship of a mightier still, before whom all powers and principalities bow down. The dead that slept here were countless; but amongst that silent host there was now but one living man, as silent and well nigh as motionless as they. It was Travers: and now he sat once again beside the grave of his dead wife. Through the long night he had kept his vigil of woe in his lonely chamber, and towards the morning's break had fallen, in the exhaustion of his physical strength, into a dull, deep, dreamless sleep, from which he had not awoke till the day was already advanced. And here he was again, drawn by the spell of his deep love, watching over the casket whence Death had stolen the jewel—the broken bowl from which the precious essence had been poured out. How impassable is the trackless gulf between the dead and the living, when Faith is not at hand to bridge it over!—how undiscernible the regions where the departed spirits abide, if no light from Revelation dispels the gloom! Faith was yet weak in the heart of Travers, and the sublime truths of Revelation had been to him hitherto but a cold and barren speculation, that exercised the powers of his reason, but touched not the springs of his affections. And hence it was that doubts and fears distracted him, and the sorrows of death compassed him round about. Did the sweet spirit that had passed away still exist in its own individuality and consciousness? would it again hold communion with his own spirit, when he, too, should lay down the flesh? or was it absorbed and lost in the great universal Spirit whence it had issued, even as the ripple sinks back upon the ocean from whose bosom it has arisen? And then his soul inquired—"How are the dead raised up, and with what body do they come?"

His heart failed him, as all these thoughts crossed his mind, and his soul found no comfort. Deep, dense clouds overcast the face of heaven, and shut out the pleasant light of the sun, and deeper clouds hung over his spirit, as he sat, in the desolation of his heart, with the sense that he had lost his treasure in this world, without the assurance that he should find it in a world to come.

"Oh!" cried he, "for some sign from heaven to resolve my doubts—to guide me through the gloom!"

At this moment the clouds, which, since morning, had hung heavily around the sun, were now riven asunder by the light breeze that sprang from the south-west, and out broke the bright sunbeams, almost from the mid-heaven, and the glorious rays shot downwards, and fell upon the gilded cross on the summit of the steeple, till it glowed like living fire; then the light went rippling, like a yellow wave, down the sloping side of the spire, till, reaching its base, it leaped across the projecting tower, and there, athwart the fresh green grave, lay the shadow of the cross!

When the mind is weakened by suffering, or overstrained by the tension of strong feeling, it is predisposed towards the supernatural. Travers received the casual illumination of the sunlight as indeed a sign from heaven—as an answer to the cry of his spirit. While he gazed in silent awe upon the grave, a voice spoke to him in solemn yet encouraging accents—"To them that sat in darkness and the shadow of death, light is sprung up."

Travers raised his eyes reverently; in his excited state of mind, he half expected to see some celestial visitant beside him. The mild, sympathising face of the young curate met his gaze.

"I have been to seek you at your lodgings, Mr.

Travers," said he; "and Dame Ashley told me you had gone out. I had little doubt where I should find you. Come, dear sir, you have indulged your grief as far as it is fitting; you must now hear the voice of the comforter."

With a gentle violence the minister constrained the mourner, and taking his arm within his own, they both went forth from the churchyard through a small turnstile that led by a path along the fields. The soft influences of spring were already beginning to be felt; the day now became brighter, for, with the noon, the clouds gradually dispersed. Buds were swelling upon the trees; the thorn and privet in the hedges were putting forth their tender, green leaves; the violet was sending up its fragrance like incense, and the daisy and primrose were specking the pastures with silver and gold; while, from the bending sprays the birds were trilling forth their songs of joy. The heart is never insensible to the sweet influences of the external world. Nature is to the physical man what God is to the spiritual man. Even the heart of Travers felt touched with a gentle complacency that was as balm to his sorrow. And now his companion spoke to him of the earthly spring— of the seed that is sown and hidden away in the earth, dying first, that it may be quickened after:

thence he led him to consider the heavenly spring—the resurrection from the dead; how that which is sown a natural body is raised a spiritual body; how it is sown in corruption, in dishonour, and in weakness, to be raised in incorruption, in glory, and in power. And so he reasoned, till, at length, the perplexed and doubting spirit found comfort and hope in the future; and, looking down into the grave, he saw its gloom penetrated by a light that shone from beyond it—the glory of that life which cometh after death.

CHAPTER V.

DEATH AND LIFE.

> "Christ ist erstanden!
> Freude dem Sterblichen,
> Den die verderblichen,
> Schleichenden, erblichen
> Mängel umwanden."
>
> GOETHE.

THE bells are chiming out with a joyous peal from the tower of the church of St. Mary's-super-Mare, and the beautiful old pile is bathed in the splendour of a cloudless morning sunshine. Groups of simple country-folk, with happy faces, and in holiday apparel, throng the churchyard, and enter through the antique porch into the nave. It is Easter-day. The service of the Church commences, and the sweet trebles of children and the deeper voices of men join in the triumphant hymn that proclaims,—"The Lord is risen!" When the service was concluded, the young curate entered the pulpit. His pale face was agitated for a moment with strong emotion, for he knew that there was amongst the congregation an auditor who came there with an anxious spirit, that looked up to him for comfort and support, and he felt the deep responsibility cast upon him to discharge his mission. The young man discoursed eloquently, for he spoke from the fulness of his heart. He told of the first Adam who was made a living man, whom all the angels of God beheld with wonder in his sinless and perfect glory—with all that was communicable of God's essence poured into him; so that Deity became visibly mirrored forth to the hierarchy of heaven. Then he narrated the sad, strange history of his fall; of his

> ——"first disobedience, and the fruit
> Of that forbidden tree, whose mortal taste
> Brought death into the world;"

and so he discoursed of death—death of the body

and death of the soul. Then he opened out the whole economy of God's dealing with man; the wondrous and merciful provision which, at the very hour of man's fall, was made for his restoration; how, at length, in the fulness of time, Death, the dread victor of the first Adam, was himself vanquished by the great quickening Spirit, the last Adam; and he spoke of that great mystery, the resurrection from the dead, as that upon which the hope of man was based—that which gave Christian philosophy its pre-eminence and perfection, and brought life and immortality to light. Passing from this theme beyond the grave, he pictured forth the things of that invisible world which the spirit of prophecy has revealed to the eye of faith; that sure and steadfast hope which is the anchor of the soul, that we shall be again united to those whom we love; that if the grave is the gate of death, death is itself the vestibule of life, beyond whose shadowy portals lie, immeasurably spread out, the regions of immortality. Travers sat behind the shadow of a pillar, eagerly drinking in the words of comfort; and, as his brow leaned against the cold stone, tears swelled up in his eyes and blinded his vision: they were the first he had shed since the hand of his dead wife lay pulseless within his own for the last time. Oh no, not for the last time; he now indeed felt there was for him a reunion beyond the grave. The life of this world shrivelled up like a scroll before his mind, while the life beyond this world expanded till it filled, as it were, the whole field of his spiritual vision. Even in this hour of his affliction his soul was elevated with a strange joy, and he felt how EASTER was, indeed, a day of glory, and of triumph, and of hope, to the Christian Church; that if the angels of God celebrated with songs of adoration and love that day whereon they led their King down from heaven, and arrayed him reverently in the panoply of flesh, and retired wonderingly, leaving him upon the battle-field to war with the two dread spiritual foes—Sin and Death—with what shouts of jubilation, and praise, and honour, did they receive again the warrior after "the noise of the battle," with "garments rolled in blood," when he had burst open the gates of hell, and destroyed the body of Sin, dragging Death captive at his chariot-wheels, and leading with him, in his triumph, thousands of liberated souls from the depths of Hades! If the Christmas hymn be one of peace and joy that "a son is born," the Easter anthem should be one of triumphant exultation that " the Lord is risen !"

And Travers passed again into the world, sobered, indeed, yet cheerful ; not broken down by sorrow, but sustained by the hope which had dawned upon his heart on that Easter-day. He looked henceforth upon life as one who must die ; upon death, as one who shall live beyond it. By degrees he gained a name and a fame ; but he sought no new alliance, ever faithful to the memory of his first love. Ere a year had passed, a chaste and simple tomb of pure marble rose over the green, grassy sods that covered the remains of his beloved. Many a year has since come and gone—the snows of Christmas and the sunshine of Easter—and he who now wanders among the graves in the churchyard of St. Mary's-super-Mare may see upon a marble slab, surmounting a tomb on the western side, the inscription :—

MILLICENT TRAVERS :

and beneath it, in letters sharper and fresher—

ALSO

FREDERICK TRAVERS, HER HUSBAND.

All Hallow Eve.

SNAP-APPLE NIGHT AT CASTLE SLINGSBY.

IF there is any zoological specimen more worthy than another of being hermetically sealed in a glass-case, or corked up in a bottle of spirits of wine, it is an old bachelor without bile or bitterness—one who is at the same time fond of children and of their grandmothers—the playfellow of the young and the counsellor of the old—who flirts with young girls, and squires old ones—who can dance, play whist, drink tea, talk scandal, or ride a foxhunt—who is all things to all men, and everything in the world to every woman. Just such a specimen is my good uncle, Saul Slingsby—the delight of all who know him for miles round—the grand projector of pic-nics and steeple-chases—a steward at every subscription ball, and *croupier* at every club dinner. How Saul escaped matrimony is a marvel to every one, for he was a good-looking and a manly fellow. I think myself that he owed his safety to the immensity of his philogyny: the lover of all womankind could never afford to incarcerate his affections within the sphere of one of the sex. Had he lived in Turkey, he would have been the happy husband of a thousand wives. But he lives in Ireland, and is, therefore, a bachelor. The Slingsbys all cluster about Uncle Saul at all the great festivals, as bees about thyme flowers, or butterflies in a sunny meadow. He is the sole survivor of a multitude of younger brothers and sisters, and has a large ancient house all to himself—as large as his heart, and as ready as that heart to take every mother's son of us into its warmest corners, and cherish us with true parental love. Of course, we all eat our apples and nuts with him; and I set out this afternoon to form one of the many friends around his festive mahogany. The day was a delicious one for the season, grey, breezeless, and full of repose; a slight, thin haze had succeeded a sharp hoar-frost, and the sun shone out with a shorn splendour; but there was a cool healthiness in the air that braced the limbs, and sent the blood flowing brisk and joyously through the veins, under the stimulus of exercise. The trees were now showing their leafless branches, exposing to view the birds' nests, which erst the summer foliage had sheltered; while here and there an odd tree still struggled to keep its leaves against frost and wind, the horse-chesnut and the elm, with their rich, sunny unber; the brown beech, the deep russet-coloured oak. How silent was all around! The fields no longer rang with the merry laughter of the reapers and corn-binders; here and there a few men and women were digging out the scant crop of diseased potatoes, but the voice of gladness did not cheer their labour; the solitary ploughman drove his horses through the stubble, breaking the silence ever and anon with his plaintive whistle; the groves were not now vocal with warblings of birds, for the winds had been busy in their leafy haunts.

"The gusts of October had rifled the thorn,
  Had dappled the woodland, and umbered the plain,"

though at intervals the note of the blackbird and the thrush broke startlingly on the ear from some still sheltered dingle. But the little house-sparrow is still hopping and twittering and chirping, and rendered more bold by the sharp winds and the nipping frosts, he comes from the hedge, and picks up the grain at the barn door; or perching on threshold and window-sills, looks timidly into the cheery rooms, and watches the movements of the inmates; or sitting on the black thorn, "pipes plaintive ditties, with a low, inward voice, like that of a love-tainted maiden, as she sits apart from her companions, and sings soft melodies to herself, almost without knowing it." I strolled along, full of pleasant fancies, and as I looked around me, and watched the lengthening shadows on hill and plain, the beautiful verses of Keble, written for this very season, came to my mind :—

> "Why blow'st thou not, thou wintry wind,
>   Now every leaf is brown and sear,
> And idly droops, to thee resigned,
>   The fading chaplet of the year?
> Yet wears the pure aerial sky,
>   Her summer veil, half drawn on high,
> Of silvery haze, and dark and still
> The shadows sleep on every slanting hill.
>
> "How quiet shows the woodland scene!
>   Each flower and tree, its duty done,
> Reposing in decay serene,
>   Like weary men when age is won.
> Such calm old age as conscience pure,
> And self-commanding hearts ensure,
> Waiting their summons to the sky,
> Content to live, but not afraid to die."

So musing, I stood, as the sun was setting, before the ancient entrance into Uncle Saul's demesne. In the apex of a semi-circle, which swept inwards from the road, rose two high, square, limestone pillars of rusticated masonry, surmounted by antique urns of the same material, but the stone, though unbroken and carefully preserved, had lost its original colour, and looked dark and weather-stained, and the tooth of time was visible in that appearance, which architects have denominated "vermiculated." From these piers swung an enormous gate of iron, the rails of which were all arrow-headed, and between the cross-bars you could see many a fantastic scroll, elaborately wrought, according to the fashion of by-gone times. At either side, the sweep of coped stonework was terminated by a pier, similar in style to those I have mentioned, beyond which stood a square, stone lodge, with a high slated roof that ran to a point in the centre, topped by a wooden ornament. I swung open one valve of the gate and passed up the long, straight, formal avenue of beech trees till I reached the house. My approach was not unnoticed, nor unannounced, for a multitude of dogs, of all sizes, ages, and species, broke out into a clamorous salutation, ranging through every note of the canine diapason, from the deep bay of the house-dog to the shrill, snappish challenge of the little, wiry-haired terrier. But I was a friend amongst that honest-hearted population, and the storm soon sank down to pleasant whinings and caressing gambols. And thus escorted, I mounted the flight of broad stone steps that led to the door of one of those fine old mansions which are still to be seen in the interior of the country—none of your gingerbread things, that you see at Kingstown and Dalkey, with their gables and gazaboes, and little windows stuck in all sorts of queer places in the roof—young Elizabethans, just come from nurse, with their white, shining faces, and flaring green-painted doors—but a noble square pile of solid masonry, not ashamed to show its honest face without a mask of whitewash upon it, pierced with innumerable windows, too narrow, I admit, for more modern taste, yet large enough withal to afford a pleasant look out for a couple of young lovers (if they cared for a look out), and to let in sunbeams and air enough for the low-ceiled rooms within. Well, the door opened, and there stood the worthy master, with outstretched hand and smiling face, welcoming "the last of the Slingsbys," for all the others had arrived before me.

I shall not trouble my readers with an introduction to all the Slingsbys, nor detail all the good things that passed into our mouths or out of them during dinner. Imagine us, then, the last dish having disappeared and the dessert laid on the table, sipping our wine and toying with the fruit in all the languid fastidiousness of sated appetite. If there is one halfhour in the twenty-four more delectable than another, believe me it is the half-hour that succeeds to a good dinner. If "the half-hour before dinner" is proverbially the most *triste* and formidable of the day, the half-hour after dinner is the most delightful. A delicious lassitude steals over the body. The beat of the pulse is full, regular, and tranquil, telling that every function plays smooth and cheerily, with as little creak or friction as the cranks and pistons of a steam-engine after the engineer has gone round them with his tin oil-can, and lubricated the joints and pivots. A pleasant haze rises around the brain, through which every external object is conveyed to the sensorium in *coléur-de-rose*, and every thought is mellowed in the intellect. And surely our after-dinner half-hour was a happy one. Jest and banter went round gleefully; incidents of former merry meetings were remembered with a smile, and the absence of some loved one, a participant of them, was noted with a sigh—aye, and a glistening tear in the eye of a fair sister or cousin! were the departed spirit watching about us, as I fondly and fully believe, those tears would be to it precious and holy. Then we had toasts and sentiments, and all the old-world fashions and gallantries of the good old times. At last some one drank to the health of Uncle Saul, coupled with the name of a once fair belle, to whom he was supposed, according to a tradition in the family, to have *almost* paid particular attentions, now a buxom widow of two defunct husbands, and as many comfortable jointures.

Saul was nearly overpowered with the roar of plaudits that followed, but he rallied with admirable dexterity. He returned thanks with great good-humour for the intended honour, which he modestly declined availing himself of, and proceeded to make a "confession of faith" upon the subject of matrimony, by which he had always been guided. "I hold it," said he, "that where parents have discharged their obligations to the state by rearing up a very large family, some of their progeny may 'take it easy,' and not push population forward too rapidly. Now in such cases I think the good old adage of 'first come first served' entitles the eldest child to rely on his privilege of primogeniture, and claim exemption from the cares and responsibilities of married life. Upon this principle I have acted, and I have no reason to complain, nor has society either; for I have vicariously rendered to it all that it could reasonably demand, in the fine family of nieces and nephews around me [great applause]. Besides, I am somewhat of Sir Boyle Roche's opinion. I don't see what posterity did for me, that I should put myself to any trouble for posterity, who, I am certain, will be very inferior, physically and intellectually, to our ancestors. So convinced am I of the constant deterioration of our species, that I would infinitely prefer, were it in my power, to reproduce my grandfather, and so turn the progress of generation back upon its source, till, becoming better and better each move, we should at last come back to our first parents, who, I have no doubt, would agitate a 'repeal of the fall,' as folks now-a-days do a 'repeal of the Union,' and with as fair a chance of success. But come, it is time to be moving, as I see the bottle has ceased to do so. I hear the fiddle in the great hall, and they want but our presence to commence the sports."

We all took the hint, and followed Saul into the apartment he mentioned. It was a room of ample dimensions, with a large fire-place midway down it, in which peat and bog-wood were blazing with a rush of flame up the ample chimney, that threw a strong red glare on the walls, and made the lights look dim and sickly. Two chairs were placed upon a table, which was drawn close to the lower-end wall, and on them were perched a fiddler and a piper, both of whom had their full complement of eyes and limbs (a thing somewhat unusual with such folk), and rather more than their full complement of strong waters within them (a thing not at all unusual in such cases). Farther up the room stood a huge tub filled with water, and from the centre of the ceiling hung the grand attraction of the night—the apparatus for the snap-apple—two cross-sticks, carrying on their points apples and candles alternately. At the other end of the room a table was well-furnished with nuts, apples, and other eatables; and upon a stool in the corner reposed a barrel of home-brewed ale, with a black-jack standing expectantly under the spigot. The servants were all in their best attire, and were standing respectfully to receive us, while two or three substantial farmers, with their wives and children, had come by express invitation to join in the merry-making. I shall not describe the games and sports of All hallow eve though, alas! the time is fast coming when they shall be matters of history, and I know no place save this where they are still maintained in their integrity. I shall however leave to our ingenious and erudite friend,

William Wilde, in some future pages of his "Popular Superstitions," to enlarge upon the subject; to tell you how the young maid steals out in the dark night to sow the hemp-seed, chaunting the spell—

> "Hemp-seed, I sow thee,
> Hemp-seed, I hoe thee,
> You that's my true love, come after and show thee;"

and then she looks fearfully over her left shoulder to see the form of him who is to be her true love; to describe the mystery of "turning the shift," and the more daring and unholy tampering with the fiend in the spell of "reeling the yarn," and saying the Lord's Prayer backwards. Let me, however, linger a moment over the pleasant and innocent pastimes of snapping apples, burning nuts, diving for money, fortune-telling and forfeits, singing songs, and telling stories, to say nothing of dancing and love-making, the former to be found at every Irish gathering, from wake to wedding—the latter at every gathering in every land since the world began. May it so continue till the world's end: indeed, the world will run a great chance of ending when this pleasant custom falls into disuse.

At a signal from Uncle Sam the sports commenced, and we were all hard at work in no time. I don't mean to recount what feats I performed—whether I caught the apple or the candle, what pretty girls I danced or flirted with, or burned as sweethearts, or how they behaved when subjected to that fiery ordeal. Fancy yourself for a moment beside me (would that you were so in reality), and look around the festive scene. See that strong, young fellow: he is the best man in the country round at throwing the sledge, and yet he cannot for the life of him catch the apple from the cross, though his great jaws open wide enough to encompass a pumpkin. There he goes again with a dash as if it were made of granite, but the apple has turned only the faster from him, and the avenging candle comes swift upon him, covering his chaps with grease and smut, and singeing his whiskers, and so he retires from the vain pursuit, for the laugh is loud against him. What chance have you, my pretty little maiden? the apple is too large for your mouth, and the flaring candle will blister that downy cheek if you fail. Well, she is trying, nevertheless. May Venus and Pomona befriend her! A mischievous rival has sent the swing twisting round like lightning. "Fair play! fair play!" cries many a manly voice; but the sly little one waits quietly till the string is now twisted almost to its utmost, and the swing is going round slower and slower, just before it changes its revolution and uncoils the cord. There now she pushes forward her little head as gently as a spaniel puts out its nose to a lady's caressing hand, and the cunning little thing has coaxed off the apple, no-body knows how, but there it is triumphantly between her red lips, looking as if it had grown together with them from the one stem. Well, leave them to their sport, and watch that girl who is binding up her rich black hair in a hard knot on the back of her head, before she dives for the shilling. Pop, in goes her head, but she raises it quickly out again with a sob and a cry, for the water has rushed into her mouth and eyes, and well-nigh choaked and blinded her; and now she lets loose her long hair, which falls down her neck and shoulders dripping with the sparkling drops, and reminding one of a mermaid, with her tresses decked with sea gems. This is a difficult feat, and few adventure it, but many are content to "bob for apples" instead; so let us pass on. You see now, "on the floor," two of the best dancers in the province at reel or jig; and the "musicianers" are playing a jig, whose galvanising powers would set a dead bear dancing, Sagart na m-buataise—"the priest of the boots," or, as it is commonly called, "the priest in his boots." There's footing for you! Talk of polkas, and mazurkas, boleros or tarantulas, quadrille or cotillon, I aver there is nothing in the world to equal an Irish jig, in the way of saltation. Mark with what exquisite accuracy the time of the air is kept by the beat of the foot, the swing of the body, the motion of the hands, and the snap of the fingers. How they "humour the tune," giving expression to every change and tone of sentiment. With what an air of bold gallantry, mingled with coaxing drollery, the young man flings his arms about the girl, as he twirls her round till her tiny feet are well-nigh lifted off the ground. How coquettishly she disengages herself, and, with a look half shy, half sly, retreats as he advances. How disdainfully she flounces round, while, imitating her example, he turns on his heel with a nonchalant air that would do credit to one of your first-rate town puppies. I aver that an Irish jig is the perfection of dancing, the poetry of motion, the drama of the feet; and if you can show me anything to compare with it, either in lordly saloons or on village greensward, then will I, Jonathan Freke Slingsby, burn my quill, break my lyre, and retire into a monastery of Trappists for the rest of my life. There now, the dance is over, and the young couple, somewhat flurried, sit down to recover their breath. Hush! look at that dark-eyed fellow, with the brown hair and black silk kerchief tied loosely round his neck: mark how he clears his throat with a cough, and stares with all his might at the ceiling, though there is not so much as a fly creeping on it. That's the surveyor, our "primo tenore;" he's going to give us a song—listen.

THE RAKE'S APOLOGY.

I.

Now hush! dearest Kathleen, give over
    Upbraiding a lover so true;
I swear, though you say I'm a rover,
    My heart is still faithful to you.
Then where is the use in your doubting,
    Or breaking my heart with your sighs;
Those sweet lips were not made for pouting,
    And anger will spoil your mild eyes.

II.

The world, dear, is given to railing,
    God forgive 'em that call me a rake;
'Tis yourself that's the cause of my failing,
    For I love the whole sex for your sake.
Sure 'tis pride of you makes me a rover
    To wake, and to dance, and to fair;
I'm still trying at each to discover
    A girl with yourself to compare.

III.

And so, just in making the trial,
    I'm forced still to touch and to taste;
Though 'tis hard, there's no good in denial,
    An hour from beside you to waste.
But their beauties leave no more impression
    Than calm waters take from the breeze;
Sit down now, and hear my confession,
    I'll make a clean breast at your knees.

IV.

Eileen Bawn has a fine neck and bosom,
    But her waist feels so tightened and *quare;*
Rose has bright eyes, but still I don't choose 'em,
    When you gaze in them long they've a stare.
Mave looks shapely and plump—'tis all dressing,
    And Norah's lips please one at *first,*
But then they won't do for much pressing,
    They're so ripe you're afraid that they'll burst.

V.

So now, all experiments over,
    I come back more faithful and true;
And I vow, on the word of a lover,
    There's no girl half so perfect as you.
Then, Kathleen, cheer up, and believe me
    I'll love you whatever betide;
One word, and that fair hand just give me,
    I'll wander no more from your side.

"Bravo! bravo!" That's a real old Irish air, and a fine one too; 'tis called "Shaun Staal," and a great favourite over the country. But we must now inspect the nut-burning; and I shall expound to you, as we look on, the manner in which auguries are taken in this mystery. A lad or a lass who wishes to learn if his or her lover will be fickle or faithful, places two nuts on the bar—one to represent the person making the experiment, the other the selected sweetheart. If the nut cracks, or jumps off the bar, the lover will prove unfaithful; if it blaze or burn, the lover will be true; and if the nuts burn both together, then is the omen the happiest of all, for the parties are sure to be married. Look closely into the faces of the young people, who are clustering anxiously round the fire at this simple divination, and you cannot fail to read the heart's history in the blush, the sigh, the eye sparkling or dimmed, the brow bright or clouded. There, too, is a love episode at the far end of the room. See that young pair, who, thinking only of themselves, know not that others' eyes are upon them. The old woman is telling them their fortune upon the cards; and a bright one it is, if we may conjecture from the happy glance of the girl and the triumphant air of the young man. But I hear Uncle Saul's voice, calling cheerily—"Come, Jack Bishop, 'tis the surveyor's call, and he has knocked you down for a song." Jack, besides his great good-humour and dramatic power, has one of the finest voices, which he manages with exquisite skill and taste, and, what is very rare with great singers, is the most obliging fellow in the world.

"With all my heart, Saul," was Jack's ready answer; "I'll give you a song of Jonathan's, to a beautiful air of Terence Magrath's—a real modern antique: 'tis called—

"MARY OF THE CURLS."

I.

As oak-leaves, when autumn is turning them sere,
Is the hue of my own Mary's beautiful hair;
And light as young ash-sprays, that droop in the grove,
Are the ringlets that wave round the head that I love.

II.

Dear Mary! each ringlet, so silken and fine,
Is a fetter that round my poor heart you entwine;
And if the wide ocean I roamed to the west,
It would still draw me back to the maid I love best.

III.

Like stars that shine out from the calm summer sky
Are the glances that beam from your melting blue eye;
Your lips red as poppies, your cheeks bright as morn;
And your bosom and neck white as blossoms of thorn.

IV.

The stars may shine down on the whole world at night,
But your eyes, Mary, dear! should give *me* all their light.
Let the poppies and blossoms be plucked by who will,
If those dear lips and bosom be kept for *me* still.

V.

Not more sportive and light is the young lambkin seen,
Than your foot in the dance on our own village green;
And my fond eye still wanders wherever you move
'Midst all the maids seeking for her that I love.

VI.

The winter is past, and the Shrovetide is nigh;
Dear Mary! no longer be cruel or shy.
I've a home to receive you, a hand to sustain,
And a heart that will love you while life shall remain.

Jack Bishop's song was received with plaudits. When the surveyor, who was a great traveller, and a very learned individual, stept forward, and said—
"I beg your pardon, Master Jonathan: but I am

thinking that's not just all out your own composing."

"Why not?" said I.

"Because, sir, 'tis mighty like an ould song they sing in the county Clare, called 'Máire na g-ciab,' which signifies in the English vernacular, 'Mary of the Curls.' I remember only the first verse of it now (and he repeated it in Irish). I think you will allow, sir, there is a very remarkable resemblance to the first verse of your song."

"Maybe so," said I.

Jack Bishop enjoyed my confusion most maliciously, but Uncle Saul covered my retreat by wishing all a pleasant night, and so we retired to the drawingroom.

"Jonathan," said my uncle, when we were all seated, "you should never pawn off a translation as an original." "Nor an original as a translation," slily interposed Jack Bishop, *sotte voce.*

Amongst the company was a little man, whom nobody seemed to know, yet he made himself very much at his ease. I first noticed him in the great hall, watching the dancers with a quiet wonder through every evolution; inspecting the divers for shillings, and mechanically opening and shutting his mouth, as if registering each snap at the apple on the twirling-cross; and all the while he spoke not a word, nor moved from his seat near the fire, till he followed us back on the invitation of Uncle Saul. Let me describe this little man for you. I will begin with his head. In shape, it resembled a pear, with the larger end downward, which was represented by a pair of fat, juicy cheeks, that hung over a white cravat, wrapt pudding-wise around his thick, short neck. His eyes were round, aud somewhat protruding, with a leaden, sleepy stare; his forehead rose conically, and bald, and over his whole face was a flush that spoke eloquently of London porter; while here and there an erubescent pimple bloomed out, whose parentage was, beyond all question, a dash of brandy, or "cold without." His body was punchy and corpulent, and covered with a yellow waistcoat, surmounted by a blue coat, with brass buttons; dark inexpressibles clothed his upper limbs, and leggings of the same colour were buttoned over his lower. "Come, Mr. Tupps," said my Uncle Saul, "what will you take?—this is excellent whiskey, or perhaps you prefer the brandy." Tupps brightened up. "The brandy, if you please, Mr. Slingsby; I rayther prefer it—they say 'tis good for the stomach. No sugar, thank you, sir, but just a leetle shade of cold water." The name "Tupps" at once solved the mystery of the little man's presence, for Saul had told me that he sold his wool in the morning to a Lancashire buyer of that name; and the little gentleman's dialect now assured me that I had the professional wool-gatherer before me.

Songs, sentiments, charades, and forfeits, having each in turn contributed to the general entertainment, at length some mischief-loving spirit put it into the heart of Saul to tamper with Mr. Tupps' taciturnity. "Mr. Tupps, the company are waiting for your song." "Well, I'm sure, sir," said Tupps, "I don't know now as how I ever sung a song in my lifetime." "Salt and water for Mr. Tupps," cried Saul. "Nay, nay, Mr. Slingsby, if a toast or a sentiment will do ——" "Well, then, Mr. Tupps, pray let us have it." Tupps replenished his glass, turned up his eyes to the ceiling, and then looking pleasantly around him, said, as he raised his glass, "'*A dry fleece and a wet skin.*' Gentlemen and ladies, your very good healths—all." A roar of laughter followed this professional sentiment. But Saul was at the little man again. "Upon my word, Mr. Tupps, that's being rather hard on the graziers; I think, however, that you are entitled to rely upon it in mitigation of punishment, and we shall be content to dispense with one-half of the penalty. Which

SNAP-APPLE NIGHT.

will you prefer, the salt or the water?" "That's Hobson's choice, sir; I'm blest if I know which to choose. Well, sir, I'll tell you a story, if you please." "Bravo!" said Saul. "Now, then, Mr. Tupps, we're all attention."

"Well, then, gentlemen," said Tupps, after he had cleared his throat with a cough, and then moistened it with a gulp of brandy and water, "I shall relate to you an adventure which once befell myself in this country, and which I shall ever look upon as a most extraordinary and providential escape. It is now over six years since I was travelling one evening in the West of Ireland, on my way to the fair of Ballybeg, which you all know is a great wool fair. There was no regular conveyance to the town, and I had hired a car at the village where the stage-coach had set me down. The road was wild and lonely, winding through a mountain-gorge, and I confess that I did not feel altogether at my ease as I sat with my back defencelessly turned to the tattered wretch who drove me, and to whom a guinea would be sufficient temptation to knock me on the head. I had a considerable sum of money about me, and my mind involuntarily recurred to all the stories of murders and robberies in Ireland, which one reads of every day in the papers. One hears a great deal, gentlemen, about 'the good old times,' but, for my part, I think that in many respects they might better be called 'the bad old times.' Roads were bad, travelling was bad, inns were bad. A man could not travel a hundred miles on his lawful calling in less than two or three days, and was obliged to take pistols and blunderbusses, and the Lord knows what, about him, as ten to one he would fall in with some Jack Sheppard or Dick Turpin by the way, who was sure to ease him of his purse, and might slit his throat into the bargain. But give me our own times—they are the real 'good times,' Free trade, a big loaf, fine inns and railroads; ay, the railroads, gentlemen, they are the grandest invention of the age. A man can now travel his couple of hundred miles between breakfast and dinner, without losing his time changing horses every ten miles, or his money, paying guards and coachmen. And then, you're so safe. To be sure you sometimes run the risk of being walked into by a runaway train, or blown up by a bursting boiler; but what is that compared to the danger which one often was in, even when I was a boy, of being encountered by highwaymen on some lonely common, having your pockets turned inside out, and your brains blown about your ears before you had time to bless yourself. He would be a smart, as well as a bold, fellow, now-a-days, who would hop over a railway-fence of a dark night, and step into the middle of the line to lie in wait for the train, and bid it 'stand and deliver,' as it comes tearing down upon him, puffing smoke and spitting fire. Well, gentlemen, to come back to my story, I was amusing myself with such pleasant thoughts as these, and, to confess the truth, they did not help much to make my mind easier. The sun had set, and the night was coming on very dark. Occasionally we passed some fellow loitering on the road side—I'm sure no good purpose brought him out at such an hour—and the driver, which I thought very suspicious, was sure to know him, and salute him with 'God save you, Mick,' or 'Good-night, Paddy.' At last, just as we turned an angle of the road at a little grove of fir-trees, two men jumped out over the ditch and ordered the driver to stop. I desired him to whip on as fast as he could, but the rascal drew up his horse in a moment. Now, ladies, you can fancy that this was enough to make any man nervous. They were stout, wicked-looking young chaps, with big sticks in their hands; and I could see, dark as the night was, something sticking out of the breast of one of their coats, that I could swear was a pistol. 'How many miles is it to Ballybeg?' asked the fellow with the pocket pistol. 'Just two from the cross-roads below there, your honour,' replied the carman. 'Well, my lad, you must give us a lift in—the gentleman will make no objection.' 'Och! not the laste in life, sir,' said the rascal, without as much as asking my leave—'Up with ye, gentlemen.' So up they got and no mistake, the fellow with the pocket pistol beside me, and the other beside the driver. I'm blest if I was not all over in a swither when I felt the fellow's breath upon me, and knew how completely I was in his power. Well, he soon began to question me, asking where I came from, what was my business, and where I meant to stop for the night. You may be sure I gave him as little information as possible, and I never felt more relieved in the whole course of my life than when we drew up at the inn at Ballybeg. The house was a small one, and it was very crowded, so I could with difficulty get accommodation, being obliged to take a bed in a double-bedded room. As I came back to have my bag fetched up, I caught a sight of the two fellows who travelled with me in conversation with the car-driver, and I heard him say, 'Oh, never fear, them sort of chaps has money enough in their pockets, I'll be bound, if a body could only get a sight of it;' these were the very words, for I shall never forget them. Well, I went into the travellers'-room, and having got a bit of something comfortable for supper, and a glass or two of grog—they had no brandy in the house, gentlemen—I went up to my bed-room. I don't know how it was, but I felt very nervous and uncomfortable, for I couldn't get the thoughts of the two ill-looking fellows out of my head. At last I went to bed, but I took care to put my pocket-book under my pillow, and left the candle lighting. I might as well have not gone to bed, for I could not get a wink of sleep; and I no sooner closed my eyes than I fancied the chap with the pocket-pistol was fumbling under my pillow for my pocket-book. I continued tumbling and turning in this way, I don't know how long, but I'm sure it could not be far from midnight, when the door opened, and what was my horror to see the two desperadoes entering on tip-toe. They looked about the room, and one of them stepped up to my bedside and peered into my face. I pretended, you may be sure, to be fast asleep, but I saw him plainly enough give a knowing wink and a smile to the other, and whisper, 'The very man, by Jupiter, and he's fast asleep.' He then examined the window, and I have no doubt in the world they intended to have got away through it after having robbed me. The other fellow had his back turned to me, but I saw him taking the pistol from his breast and lay it on the table. 'That driver is a prime lad,' said he, 'I got a full charge of the right sort from him.' 'That's lucky,' said the other, 'and now to business; the house is quiet, and *'tis just the time for taking notes.*' Ladies and gentlemen, I felt that the critical moment which was to decide my fate had arrived. I seized my pocket-book, sprang out of bed, and flinging my inexpressibles across my arm, I darted out of the door, which I closed after me, and gained the kitchen, I know not how, in safety. My first notion was to fly from the house, but the rain was coming down in torrents, and I should be certain to lose my life if I went out half-naked in the wet and cold. Fortunately I saw a settle-bed in the corner, which was unoccupied. I locked the door, stirred the fire, and threw myself in the settle, holding my pocket-book in one hand and my inexpressibles in the other, to be prepared for any emergency. Strange to say, I fell asleep, in spite of all my endeavours to keep awake. At length I was aroused by a violent knocking at the door, and a woman's voice calling out, 'The divil take you, Lanty, what's come over you at all, to be locking yourself in that-a-way?

Open the door, I tell you.' I rose, and found the day had just broken; so, slipping on my inexpressibles, I opened the door, and the housemaid bolted in upon me. 'Wisha, the divil take —— Oh, the Lord between us and harm! who are you at all?' cried the girl, starting back. I explained to her that I had come down to sleep in the kitchen, as I had a great objection to occupy a room with strangers, and begged her to step up to No. 15, and fetch me my clothes. Off she went, and returned in a few moments with my apparel, saying, 'Why, sir, there's nobody at all in the room; the two gentlemen that slept in the big bed went away just now.' Well, you may be sure I felt thankful for my extraordinary deliverance from the villians, who, it was plain enough, had decamped before any one was stirring, having the fear of the bridewell before their eyes. I returned to the room and finished my sleep; but I thought it the wisest course to say nothing about what happened in the night, as the landlord might say I was injuring his house, and bring me into trouble. And now, ladies and gentlemen, I think you will agree with me in saying this was a very singular adventure."

During Mr. Tupps's narrative, his auditory were all attention; but had any one looked at Bishop or myself he would have seen amazement depicted on every feature of our faces. Jack now advanced towards Mr. Tupps, and, beckoning me forward, we stood before him. Looking fixedly in his face, Jack said, "Pray, Mr. Tupps, did you ever see us before?" The little man looked long and bewilderedly in our faces. At length he said, "Well, I'm blest now—no, it can't be—yes, it is. Why, upon my credit you are very like the fellows—ahem! I beg pardon, the individuals—who thought to—a—a—who travelled into Ballybeg with me." "The very identical fellows, Mr. Tupps, as you are pleased to call us—wicked-looking fellows—ill-looking dogs. Eh, sir?" "Well but, gentlemen, I really did not know you were present; besides, you had terrible beards and whiskers then, and you wore no shirt-collars. But, indeed, I cannot understand the thing at all. Were you not really highwaymen?" "Pray, sir, say that again," said Jack, looking most comically ferocious; "I did not exactly hear the word you made use of." "Nay, sir, I mean no offence, I assure you; but, perhaps you'll be so kind as to explain the matter, for I'm blest if I know what to think." "That's easily done. My friend and myself were making the tour of the western counties on foot, and were fortunate enough to meet your car, so as to get a 'lift' into Ballybeg. The only room left at the inn was the one in which we were all put, and having paid our bill at night, we were off in the morning by daybreak. I confess we were quite unable to account for your bolting so suddenly out of the room, but we thought you had been asleep, and had gone out in a fit of somnambulism." "Well, well, but what do you say about your conversation with the car-driver?" "Why, he was complaining that you declined to give him any gratuity." "And so I did, because he took you up without my leave. What did you mean by saying that the driver had given you a charge of the right sort?" "Oh, the fellow was grateful for a few shillings we gave him, and put me in the way of filling my 'pocket-pistol' with some genuine potheen whiskey." "Dear, dear! how strange. Well, there's but one thing more which, if you can clear up, I shall admit that I wronged you. Why did you say that it was just the hour for taking notes? Can you deny that you said these very words, sir?" "Ha! ha! ha!" shouted Bishop. "Mr. Slingsby must explain that to you; he is answerable for having unkennelled you." "That I will," said I. "You must know, sir, that we were in the habit of keeping a journal of our tour, and made it a practice to note down whatever had occurred to us worthy of remark during the day. I assure you, Mr. Tupps, you occupied a very considerable portion of our diary that night."

The shame and confusion of Mr. Tupps was now complete. I thought he would have sunk into the earth. At length Uncle Saul, in pity to his sufferings, came to the rescue. "Upon my word, Mr. Tupps, I do not at all wonder at your having fallen into the mistake you did. I am sure I should have been very much frightened if I were in your place. You showed admirable presence of mind to decamp with your baggage, and in good order. And now I will give you a song myself, and you must all fill your glasses to pledge me in the toasts, and join in the chorus."

After Uncle Saul's song, 'twas near the "small hours," and so ended our "ALL HALLOW EVE."

The Feast of All Souls.

THE COUNT OF CASTEL VECCHIO.

CHAPTER I.

TRAVELLERS' FARE.

ONE cannot readily imagine a wilder or more desolate spot than the rude inn or post-house of Monteroni, that stands, or stood some thirty years ago, midway between Rome and Civita Vecchia. I had left the Eternal City at noon, and lumbered across the savage and solitary wastes that stretch westward along the ancient "Via Aurelia," and thence by the desolate sea-shore, in one of the worst *vetturas*, having as my companions an elderly invalid gentleman and his daughter, both English. The former was a type of his class, grave, and rather taciturn, with a profound contempt for everything that was not English, and venting his querulous observations on bad roads, slow travelling, and villanous culinary compounds, the miserable substitutes for the roast beef of home. The young lady was a genuine disciple of the school of romance, which British boarding-schools and French novels have produced in great abundance, with a pale face, blue eyes, full and pensive, and profusion of rich brown hair. Night fell around us chill and cheerless—for it was November—ere we reached the inn where we were to pass the hours till morning. When we entered, through the stable, the only sitting-room which the house afforded—half kitchen, half coffee-room—three or four peasants were seated loungingly at a large table, consuming a homely supper of dark bread, grapes, and fish, to which were added some flasks of the *vino dell paese*, which, to say the truth of it, is in that region execrable enough. The looks of these fellows were anything but agreeable, though sufficiently picturesque. They eyed us with a rude gaze, and then resumed their occupation; and, as they hewed large slices off the loaf with their long, sharp-pointed clasp knives, that served alike for the purpose of life and death as occasion required, and conversed with each other in a rough, rude jargon, unlike the soft accents which we had been accustomed to hear from the *Bocca Romana*, one could not help associating them with the bandits and cut-throats that at no very distant period filled the Campagna di Roma, to the terror of all peaceable travellers. Some thoughts of this sort seemingly passed through the mind of the Englishman, and were still more evidently pourtrayed on the intelligent face of his daughter. In a short time their repast was finished, and they rose, stretched their huge limbs, yawned, braced the thongs that bound their leggings, and stuck their clasp knives in their sashes, while one of the party threw a few silver pieces on the table. These a dirty dishevelled *ragazza* picked up, and, handing them their change, consisting of some small copper coins, they departed, without taking further notice of us, to our infinite satisfaction. Meantime the girl removed the *debris* of the peasants' supper, swept the table with a towel, flung over it a linen cloth, coarse, and not over clean, and placed knives, spoons, and horn drinking-cups—the scanty and hasty preparations for our meal.

In a few moments more, a huge ladle had drawn up, from a caldron that smoked over the fire, a liquid which one better skilled in such things than I am would find it difficult to classify under an appropriate head in the department of gastronomy. A Frenchman would call it *soup maigre;* an Englishman would pronounce it greasy water: a dog would have suspected that it was the washings of dishes, with an undue quantity of the aqueous element super-added; at all events, a fair analysis would have detected the presence of animal substance, infinitesimally diluted, together with a liberal admixture of meal, vegetables, and herbs of a strong and unsavory odour. I was hungry and cold, tolerably young then—for, alas! it is a great many years ago—and had a strong stomach, and was well used to rough fare, so I contrived to swallow down a fair share of the composition.

My male companion, encouraged by my performance, essayed a spoonful—aye, and got it down; but his powers of endurance could go no farther, and, with an exclamation graced with an English expletive that I need not repeat, he thrust the plate at arm's length from him. The young lady looked at her share with an expression of distress so ludicrously piteous, that I could scarce refrain from laughing outright. This was our first course. Next came, from the same teeming vessel that supplied the *soup*, a mass of flesh, which might have been beef, or might not—I am not Tartar enough to pronounce upon horse-flesh, and, certes, the fibres of a nice young colt, if boiled for two hours or so, might have been as tender. This was distributed amongst us, and, in order to make it more tempting, oil, vinegar, pepper and mustard were laid before us. In a frenzy of desperation, the old gentleman turned upon some fish, bread and cheese, which were now produced, and, calling for the best wine that the house afforded, washed down his meagre supper with a draught or two. The girl contrived to procure a few grapes and figs, which, being the production of Nature, were at least palatable. While we were thus engaged, the sound of wheels and the tinkle of horse-bells were heard without, and in a few minutes we were joined by two others. They were travellers like ourselves—the one a man of, it might be, about five-and-thirty, to judge from his figure, and the raven blackness of his hair and moustache; but the sharp, worn appearance of his features, and the baldness of his high, pale forehead, told either of more years or of something that made each year count double: the last seemed the more probable, from the wild restlessness of his sunken and brilliant eyes, that contrasted touchingly with a melancholy languour that overspread his visage. His companion was a short, thickset, and remarkably strong man, with a frank, placid countenance, and, to judge from his manner—at once respectful yet familiar—he seemed to occupy the position of a favoured though inferior companion. The former seated himself at the table, after a courteous salutation of our party, and the second very methodically proceeded to the inexhaustible cauldron, and took upon himself to inspect the contents.

The result seemed to be unsatisfactory in the extreme, for he flung back the ladle with an emphasis that sent the liquid splashing and hissing into the fire, and, uttering a thoroughbred Gallic *Sacre-e-e!* that did our hearts good, walked out of the room.

In a short time he returned with a little packet in his hand, and seizing a small earthen vessel, filled it with hot water; he then threw in a square of portable soup, and, in a moment, set a plate before his companion, which exhaled an odour that was at once tantalizing and refreshing.

This done, he once more took the ladle, and, fishing up the nondescript flesh, sat down leisurely at a little distance, and commenced his own supper. The other now, for the first time, broke the silence observed amongst us.

"I fear," said he, and his speech showed he was a Frenchman, "you have fared but badly, unless you had the good fortune to have made some provision beforehand."

"Infernally," said the old gentleman; "it is a choice between starvation and poison."

"Let me offer you something that will insure you against either fate," replied the unknown. "Pierre has a few more cakes of soup left, which, as we shall be at Rome to-morrow, we can spare."

The offer was accepted by the old gentleman and his daughter. For myself, I had contrived to satisfy my wants in the way of eating, and declined.

By degrees we fell into conversation, as travellers, when they meet, are wont to do. The stranger's observations were acute and lively, but had, withal, something eccentric about them; and he passed rapidly from one subject to its very opposite—from a gay jest to a pathetic reflection—with a facility and frequency that showed a mind as restless as it was inquisitive. And now our Hebe produced coffee, which Pierre took upon himself to prepare, and in a few minutes we had each a cup of *cafe nero* as warm and fragrant as heart could desire. Having inspected our sleeping apartments, and found them as desolate as the principal chamber, the Englishman and I returned to the *salon*. The wind, meantime, had risen to a gale, and came in gusts wild and sudden, beating against the windows till they rattled and creaked, while, at intervals, the surges of the not distant sea broke on the ear in low and melancholy moanings. The fire sank lower in the huge chimney, and a sense of cheerlessness was creeping through the large gloomy chamber. The hour of retiring had arrived, but none of us seemed disposed to seek the solitude of our chambers in so wild a night and so cheerless a house. The old gentleman wrapped his travelling cloak around him, and shawled his daughter closely. The stranger arose and walked to and fro, and Pierre poked out some faggots which he flung on the fire, for the girl had gone to her bed.

"What a terrible night!" said the old gentleman.

"Aye, aye. The wind has glorious gambolling around the old gables," said the unknown excitedly. "How I love such a *tantamarare*."

"The lonliness is quite depressing," said the young lady, looking timidly around her. "One is reminded of the 'Castle of Otranto' and the romances of Mrs. Radcliffe, and expects to see bandits or ghosts gliding out of those dark recesses."

"Ghosts! ghosts!" said the unknown, in a wild, tremulous voice; "who expects to see ghosts?"

"Nay," said I, "none here, I hope; for myself, I have no such expectation, as I do not believe in such visitants."

"Do you not?" responded he quickly; I do, for I have seen ghosts—aye, hundreds of them."

"I will not dispute any man's experience," said I, "and when I shall see, I too shall believe."

There was a pause of a few moments, during which the stranger's eyes gleamed with a restless and turbid light, and his lips moved as if communing with himself. Then he said aloud to me, in answer to my last observation—

"I could tell you a tale to remove your scepticism;" at the same time time looking furtively around, as if in search of some one.

"Perhaps, then, you will favour us with the narration. I can scarcely imagine a more fitting time or place; and, as Mademoiselle seems as little inclined for retiring as ourselves, I dare say she will have no objection."

The young lady assented with anxious alacrity; even the old gentleman showed symptoms of curiosity.

So we all prepared to listen.

CHAPTER II.

THE RIDE BY MIDNIGHT.

"WELL then," said the Frenchman, "you must know that last year I chanced, when in Germany, to make the acquaintance of a young Sicilian nobleman——"

At this moment Pierre, who had been absent from the room seeing to his master's accommodation for the night, re-entered. The unknown suddenly became silent, as he caught the eye of Pierre fixed upon him. The expression of the man's countenance was singular, and, to me, inexplicable. It seemed that of remonstrance, almost stern, yet melancholy and respectful. He uttered not a word, but his master responded to the look, whose language he seemed to understand.

"Nay, good Pierre, it must be so; I cannot sleep, and it will do us all good. Do not thwart me, I pray you."

The other sighed, and seemed to submit, though evidently with no good will. The ghost-seer then continued.

"The Sicilian and I soon became intimate, and our intimacy ripened into friendship; for he was one to love. Frank, light-hearted, and high-spirited, the world was all sunshine to him, for he knew no care and he had no want. He was the son of the old Count of Castel Vecchio, one of the wealthiest nobles of the island, whose estates lay along the rich plain of Catania, and being an only child, he had the prospect, at no distant day, of inheriting an ample independence. We proposed rambling together through Switzerland and Italy, and then visiting his paternal estates, to which he cordially invited me. Intelligence of the sudden and dangerous illness of the old Count frustrated our plans, and my friend hurried homewards, first exacting from me a promise that I would meet him in Sicily, and be present at his marriage with a Neapolitan lady, whom he was engaged to espouse in the ensuing winter. Meantime, I pursued my wanderings alone. At Geneva, I again heard from my friend, announcing the death of his father almost immediately on his arrival, and pressingly renewing his invitation. From the young Count I did not hear again; a circumstance that gave me no uneasiness, as the uncertainty of my movements precluded communication. I loitered through the summer and autumn in the beautiful scenes of Helvetia and Italy and at length, upon the first of November, I found myself in the town of Catania. A few hours brought me to the residence of my friend, an ancient pile, as its name denoted, strongly fortified, and buried amid the gloom of pine woods, that, even at this season, cast the shadows of their dark-green foliage athwart the heavy towers and deep moats.

As I drove into the large court-yard, beneath the heavy archway of black and frowning masonry, there was an air of solitude which surprised me. No attentive menials came forward to meet me, and the loud echoing baying of an old hound was the only answer to the clang of the horse's hoofs on the pavement. I descended from my carriage, and rang more than once at the massive oaken door, when at length a white-headed servitor appeared, and, to my inquiries, stated that the Count was at home, and then leading me to the saloon, retired with my card to inform his master. As I looked around me, there was, I scarce knew what, that chilled and disheartened me. The room was in disarray. A walnut escritoire lay open, at which some one had evidently been recently writing, and on a table beside were piles of old deeds and papers, while in a corner of the room stood a large chest, strongly corded, and near it trunks, valises, and travelling bags. I had scarcely time to make this survey when the door opened, and my friend threw himself into my arms.

"'*Enrico carissimo, come mi rallegro di rivederti?*' cried

he, with a warmth that told me there was no change in his heart, at all events.

"'Dear Ferdinand, I embrace you with my whole heart!' and I pressed him again, with the love of a brother. But how is this?' said I, after a moments survey. 'You are not well, my friend. Where is your bright smile and your gay looks? Has aught befallen since I heard from you?'

"'Sit down, dear friend,' said he, 'and share my sorrows, as you have heretofore shared my joys.'

"My heart sank at his words, as I flung myself on a fauteuil beside him.

"'You know of my father's death, Henry,' commenced my friend, 'but you know not, nor indeed did I when I wrote to you, the sad results that have followed it. Listen, then, to my story; though a sad, it will be a brief one. I hurried here, after parting from you, with the utmost speed, to find, alas! my dear father in the last extremity. A shock of paralysis had struck him down; he knew me, but was unable to speak, though he made most pitiable efforts to do so, for something was evidently lying heavily on his mind, which he sought to disclose—but in vain: he soon became insensible, and he died the next day. After I had discharged the last duties to my parent, and investigated my affairs, I found, from memoranda in his hand-writing, that I was a beggar. An unfortunate passion for gambling had of late taken possession of my father, and totally absorbed him. He lost portions of his estates, one after another, and at length, a few days before his death, he staked his all, even the castle in which we now sit, in a desperate attempt to repair his fortunes, and lost. A nobleman of Messina, whose success in gaming has been the surprise of all who knew him, won the last remnant of our paternal lands. My father signed the fatal deed that made it over for ever, returned home, and was seized with the attack that terminated his life; and, strange to say, the winner did not long survive him. I was soon called upon to resign to a stranger the home of my ancestors. I thought to impugn the deed—but in vain, for there was no one living to throw light on the transaction. And now, dear Henry, what remains for me but to seek some honourable means of living? To-morrow I leave this Castle, and with the remnant of my fortune, and the sale of family jewels, I mean to try a soldier's life.'

"'And your marriage, my poor friend?' said I.

"'I have voluntarily relinquished an alliance that was the dearest wish of my heart. It would be dishonourable to pursue it.' 'Well, well,' he resumed cheerily, after a thoughtful pause, 'it becomes not a young heart and a strong arm to despair. *Aide toi et le ciel t'aidera* is the hopeful proverb of your country. Come, I have something still in the old chateau to refresh a friend, and you must be weary after your travel.'

"After our repast, we wore away the hours in devising schemes for the future, and midnight was approaching when I sought repose. The chamber to which I was conducted was in one of the wings of the castle, with a large window looking out northward. The walls were hung with tapestry, save one end, which was panelled with dark oak, in the centre of which hung a full-length portrait. I raised the light to examine it, and saw that it was a cavalier in the prime of life, mounted on a black charger. The face and figure bore a strong resemblance to those of my friend, and the eye glowed with the fire of life, and seemed to follow me with an intense gaze as I moved from side to side. I know not how long I gazed, as if fascinated, and at length, throwing a few billets of wood in the ample grate, I flung myself on the bed, without undressing. The night was wild and wintry, and dark clouds scudded over the heavens, through which the watery rays of the full moon, from time to time, struggled with a fitful illumination. The agitating recital I had just heard banished sleep from my eyes, and, as I looked through the chamber, the logs blazed up suddenly, and threw their flickering light on the picture opposite me, till I almost fancied, as the glare played upon it, that the eye kindled and the features moved. Midnight pealed out while I thus watched in a sort of dreamy reverie, unable to withdraw my eyes from the portrait. I cannot say what time passed thus, till I closed my eyes in very weariness. A ringing sound, as of the champing of a bit when the bridle rein is drawn, suddenly aroused me, and in the dubious light I beheld the cavalier dismount from his steed, and approach the bed. I gazed in mute terror on the wild yet melancholy face; then, recovering from the horror that bound my senses, I said, 'In heaven's name, who are you, and what is your mission?'

" 'It is not too late yet,' said the figure, in a hollow voice. 'Know you that this is the Eve of All Souls? Arise and come with me.'

"A spell was on me that I could not resist; I arose. The cavalier stept back towards the horse, his cold black eyes still fixed upon me. 'Mount,' said he. I obeyed mechanically. The figure sprang up behind me, and, seizing the rein, shook it impetuously. The steed sprang wildly forward with a start, as if struck with the spur, and, bounding through the window that yielded to his touch, his iron hoofs the moment after rang upon the payment in the court-yard. A gust of wind swept howling by us, the huge valves of the oaken gate swung open, and we dashed through the troubled moonshine into the dark forest of pine trees. The night air blew on my brow refreshingly, and my first feelings of terror became overmastered or absorbed in a state of intense and sublime excitement. I know not how to describe my sensations, I was, as it were, in a new and higher existence, and in a subtler element. Every corporeal sense seemed endowed with keener powers of perception, and my mind became suddenly expanded and elevated, as gas mounts and dilates when the pressure is removed from it. I saw every thing at a glance; I comprehended every thing as by intuition. I felt a strange struggle of contending principles, that made the blood rush wildly from the heart to the brain, and back again — a sort of ecstasy that was neither wholly pleasure or pain, delight or awe, but an unblending combination of each of them. For a time our course was through the dark and tangled wood, and we sped forward, unchecked by fallen trees or dense brushwood, the glimpses of the moonshine now glinting on us through the openings of the forest, and, anon, the darkness shrouding us in its ebon mantle. Then we emerged upon the open plain; when, lo! right before us rose in the distance the cone of the mighty Monte Gibello, puffing up into the heavens its sulphury breath.

The rank grass lay in luxuriant vegetation, even at this season, beneath the hoofs of the wild horse, but his feet brushed swiftly over it, as lightly as those of the grasshopper in the summer, as, with out-stretched neck, and dilated nostril, he seemed to devour the space that lay before us. A small, bright stream ran winding through deep pasture land, glittering in the moon-beams like a silver snake. One bound, and we were at its margin— another, and it was left behind, and I heard but for a moment the gurgling song of its waters.

And now our path became broken, for the surface of the ground undulated in knolls and dells. We approached the base of Etna, passing in our transit hamlets and shepherds' huts. How lovely, even in this hour of night, was the scene around! The acclivity hung like a vast expanded garden of primæval nature. Surpassingly beautiful shone the landscape, as in a troubled sleep—light and shadow flitting over its features, as the soul hovers in dreams over the face of a sleeping child. The orange and the lemon trees still were arrayed in their golden fruit, the pomegranates flung their fragrance around, and the vines waved their graceful branches in the night breeze—while the fair bosom of the earth shone with jewel-flowers of a thousand hues. A sound came on the wing of the wind. It was the solemn clang of the convent bell from a neighbouring grove of Ilex; and, as the holy pealing passed athwart us, I felt the steed tremble from neck to flank, and start forward with a new and wild energy. Away—away—still climbing upwards. The romantic loveliness of the garden clime is left behind and below; the odour of fruit and flower comes faint upon the senses, but the sultry breath of the bituminous volanco taints the air. Now we skirt groves of chesnuts, poplars, and cork-trees; anon, we plunge into a dense forest of oak, beech, and pine. Then we tread crashingly amid a gloom and waste of black lava, like streams arrested and charred in their course by the blighting spell of a demon. With dash and strain we reeled onwards, over the black shingles, into a dark and desolate ravine, stretching upwards and onwards, spurning the scarped rocks, whose sides looked as if vitrified by the fire-flood that from the world's birth had poured over them. And then we emerged upon a wild, trackless, solitary desert heaped up steeply into the sky—a sublime, solemn mountain of ashes, piled in mournful and appalling grandeur around the crater of Monte Gibello. Oh, sublime majesty of nature! How my soul absorbed thy wondrous and fearful beauty, as it were without the aid of the dim, dull, tardy senses of the body. Time seemed expanded, as if seconds discharged the work of years. Space seemed contracted and crushed together for my spirit-vision, till I saw the smallest and nearest objects, the mightiest and most distant, crowded together, and yet unconfused before me. The dark sea rolled far off, eastward, rippling against the distant promontories of Calabria; while, inland, stretched around us, the forest belts that we had pierced through, the mighty torrents of lava that streaked and cauterised the mountain sides; and, lower still, the sweet villages, the church spires, and the sylvan huts lay sleeping securely, with cattle browsing on the rich tranquil pastures, and by the sides of gleaming waters. Overhead, the moon rushed through the masses of billowy clouds—now swallowed up in their dark volumes, now bursting out among the patches of blue sky—speeding on like a storm-tossed vessel through the boiling ocean. Onward and upward still! through the ashes that flew from the feet of the horse as the light sand on the desert, till the hot and sulphurous breath of the crater swept stiflingly upon my forehead. There, in the solemn night, the inner life of the world was struggling out of its mighty body—the soul of one of the leviathans that swim through the ocean of space mounting up to the great creative soul of the universe. A lurid light, mingled with the dusky vapour that rolled up from the throat of the mountain, and a dull muffled roar, like the breathings of a thousand furnace-blasts, issued from the depths below. Onward and upward no more; for the steed stands on the narrow crust of the crater's edge—one gaze on the glorious expanse of heaven—one glance at the gleaming sea and the beautiful earth—one, and no more! With a bound and wild snort, the black steed plunged headlong downwards. The fuliginous waves of vapour boil around me, strangling my breath, and forcing my eyeballs to start from their sockets. Stifling heat, and the glow of red carbon amid the darkness of hell—the splash of scalding water, and the shower of blinding ashes. All these I perceived for a moment, with intense and vivid distinctness; and then—the nothingness of the death-trance!"

CHAPTER III.

THE POTION.

The Frenchman paused suddenly in his strange narrative. From the time that he commenced the description of his wild midnight ride, he had become gradually more and more excited by the subject. His eyes moved restlessly at times, and then were fixed, with a wild, dilated glare, as on some object that filled their whole vision. Perspiration stood in perceptible moisture on his forehead, he breathed hard and hurriedly, and he spoke with a nervous and agitated manner, and in a voice that, at times, sank to a low impressive whisper. At last, as he described the fatal bound into the crater, he actually seemed to us all to be undergoing the suffering which he described, and, as he ceased to speak, I expected to see him swoon away.

The effect of his story on his auditory was different, according to the age and temperament of each. The elderly gentleman was at first phlegmatic and listless, then he stared at the narrator more in amazement than from interest in the tale, till at last, when the speaker stopped, he said, half-aloud—

"Bless my soul! I never saw so strange a person in my life."

The young lady was quite a study. With head inclined forward and lips apart, she devoured the wondrous narrative. Her blue eyes filled with tears at the Count's misfortunes; she sighed, shuddered, and trembled by turns, and, when the terrible catastrophe was suddenly announced, she shrieked outright.

For myself, I had heard and read so many surprising things in my wanderings about the world, for the truth of all of which there was ever some one or other ready to do battle or stake his existence, if necessary; and I had, besides, more than once, seen with my own eyes and heard with my own ears what, if these organs had not deceived me most scandalously, transcended the limits of ordinary credulity; so that I learned to suspend, as much as possible, my credence, without taking upon me to discredit any man's assertions. In short, I adopted, though perhaps in a different spirit, the sentiment of our own Wordsworth, that

> "He is oft the wisest man
> Who is not wise at all."

There was another auditor, if such he may be called, —I mean Pierre. When his master began his narrative, the man, with an air of quiet resignation, thrust his hand into a capacious pocket in the breast of his coat, whence he drew forth a round and shallow *papier mâché* box, on the lid of which was a soiled and scratched picture of two Flemish boors sitting sociably with their pipes and tankards. Opening the box, he took out a piece of tobacco, and proceeded with great deliberation to cut it in small pieces, which he then rubbed together in his hands. This done, he took from the same pocket a stained meerschaum, with a short stem of cherry-wood—it was, no doubt, his greatest solace of life, so he kept it always next to his heart. This he filled with tobacco, and then returning to the fireside, he lit his pipe, and betook himself leisurely to the beatitude of smoking. What his contemplations were, if any, it would be hard to divine, for the outward man was all repose, save the puffs of smoke that, at regular intervals, curled from the corner of his mouth. His master's tale, if it reached his senses at all, failed apparently to move him in any way. Once, indeed, when the former, in describing the clang of the horse's hoof on the pavement of the castle courtyard, smote his hands sharply together, Pierre looked up at him with a long inquisitive inspection; then, rising from his seat, he left the room, and returned in a few minutes with a small leathern case and a vessel of water. The tranquillity of his smoking process was, however, incurably disturbed, and he glanced from time to time at his master, as the excitement of the latter increased, till, at the moment when the young lady uttered the scream, which I have already recorded, Pierre arose, poured some water into one of the drinking-horns, and, taking from the leathern case a little phial, he dropped into the water a small quantity of dark brown liquid, and, stepping over to his master, handed the cup to him to drink.

"Prenez en, Monsieur," said he, in a tone which partook of chagrin, as well as of commiseration. "Ah, mon Dieu! I knew well how it would be."

The master took the cup in silence, and swallowed its contents. In a moment he revived, and soon became composed, and turning with a kind smile to the servitor, said—

"Nay, good Pierre, it is nothing. I am quite well again, you see."

Pierre made no reply, but, taking the cup from his master's hand, replaced it on the table; but, as he returned to his nook by the chimney, I could hear him grumbling to himself—

"*Que je suis sot de le permettre; mais que peut on dire au—*" The last word of the sentence was lost in the distance, and went up the chimney with the smoke.

Common civility required that we should all apologise for being in some sort the cause of disturbing our strange companion. We expressed our regret, and added our entreaties that he would not resume a narrative which had already moved him so deeply. But, while the old gentleman and I did so with entire sincerity, I thought the entreaty of our fair companion, though full of tenderness and pity, was not as pressing as it might have been. In fact, I suspected her of a desire to hear all the remaining horrors of the story, which was too strong to be overcome even by her own excitement, or that of the narrator.

"Nay, indeed, Monsieur," said the girl, "you must not distress yourself for our gratification. Though your tale is wonderfully interesting, still I should be sorry to——"

She was quickly relieved from any fears or scruples which she might have entertained, by the Frenchman saying, in a tone of impatience that precluded all further interference on our parts—

"Pray say no more about the matter, or you will distress me. I do not mean to retire for some time, as I know I should not sleep; besides," he continued, looking at Pierre, "I *must* finish what I have begun."

We offered no longer any opposition, and our companion, after a few moments of silence, resumed his tale. The draught which Pierre had administered operated most powerfully in composing both the mind and body of the Frenchman. His voice was now low, gentle, solemn, even plaintive, and the train of thought that introduced the next scene of his extraordinary narrative harmonised with the tones in which he spoke.

CHAPTER IV.

HADES.

"Who is there that believes that the soul of man, when it leaves its tenement of clay, visits not again the scenes of its former joys and sorrows? Who, that ever cherished father or mother, kinsfolk or friends, even as himself—that loved some beautiful being dearer still than his own soul—who, when they are ravished from him, could bear up against the weight of his sorrow, did he not believe that those beloved spirits moved about him—that they were the warmth in the sunbeams that makes his heart lighter, the freshness in the breeze that cools his aching temples—that they hover about him in the stillness of night, and manifest themselves to his spiritual eyes in visions that the clouded senses of the body cannot appreciate? How gladly do we turn from the cold delusions of the living to the mystic realities of what men call the dead. How immeasurably happier are we in our spiritual converse with the disembodied than in our intercourse with those whose souls we cannot see, for the impenetrable walls of their dark prison-house. And then, as they soothe our sorrows, so can we assist to lighten their sufferings. As they prayed with us, and for us, while in the flesh, so now pray we for them, while in their spiritual purgation. Such is the faith of our Church, though I know many of you Anglican reformers hold it to be 'a fond thing vainly invented.' Have you never heard how, near a thousand years ago, a pious monk of Clugny left his cloister, and toilfully journeyed over land and sea, till he reached the holy city where his Heavenly Master died; and when he had fasted and wept and prayed on Calvary, he turned his steps homeward again. The hand of heaven guided his course, so that he passed through Sicily in his route. He was one who pried into the hidden things of nature, for his spiritual senses were not obscured by fleshly indulgence, and so he was impelled by a strong desire to see Mount Etna, and witness the majesty of God in the fire and brimstone of the nether world, as he had seen it in the thunder and lightnings of heaven, in the storms on the sea, and the shakings of the earth. It was on the feast of All Saints that he toiled up the mountain sides, and night had fallen on him before he reached its summit. At length, when it was past midnight, he stood on the edge of the dark gulf which the tradition of the country believed to be the mouth of Hades. It was a calm, still night, and the mountain lay in dark repose; a thin vapour alone told of the fires that slumbered within. Then the monk heard the sounds of wild wailing, and groans, mingled with cursings. But his heart was bold and his faith strong, and he crossed himself devoutly, and prayed to Him in whom the devils believe and tremble. Then he listened attentively, and after a little while he could distinguish words, and he became spiritually cognizant of their meaning, and, though he was full of awe and wonder, yet he rejoiced exceedingly. They whose voices he heard were the evil spirits, the enemies of mankind, and they howled with rage and impotent malice against the holy monks of his own monastery of Clugny, because that their prayers and supplications had wrested from the powers of those evil ones many souls of the departed. Then the good monk returned on his way full of thanksgiving and joyfulness, and when he reached his own country he related to his abbot—whose name was Odilo—all that he had heard. Thereupon the abbot questioned him as to the day when this happened, and finding it was on the morning of the 2nd of November, he straightway appointed that the anniversary of that day should be ever after observed in his monastery, and he ordained that prayers should be made thereon for all departed souls. And so it was continued, till in later times the Pope established it to be a general holiday throughout the Christian world, as the '*Commemorazione dei fideli defonti.*'

"When consciousness returned to me I found myself lying by the bank of a wide and dark rolling river. The scene around me was wild and gloomy. A region arid and desolate stretched beside and behind me, shut in by steep inaccessible mountains, upon which no verdure bloomed. All was savage solitude—no living thing was within ken of my eye. As my sight became familiar with the darkness, I descried beyond the broad river a red twilight, as of distant fires glowing upon a sterile plain that stretched far away beyond my vision. By degrees I perceived this plain was thronged with pale spectral forms, flitting restlessly to and fro as the bleak winds swept them about. Then faint, and solemn, but in tones of unspeakable sweetness, came down, as from the upper world, the chanting of earthly voices, and I recognised the sublime sentences of our Church, assigned to the service for the departed souls of men—

'*Justorum animæ in manu Dei sunt, et non tanget illos tormentum malitiæ. Visi sunt occulis insipientium mori, illi autem sunt in pace.*'

"As these words floated in the air, the spectral beings ceased to move about, and stood listening, their pallid and anguish-marked faces turned upwards in the mute agony of supplication, and I felt that the prayers of the just were ascending to heaven in urgent entreaties for those who were undergoing the trial of the purgatorial flames. Then I beheld the faces of many of those shadows brighten, and the flames glowing less fiercely around them, while the black stains upon their forms waxed fainter. But others knew no remission of their sufferings from the holy strain: the sin-marks spotted them as darkly as before, and the flames wrapped them with unabated fury. While I gazed in breathless wonder, a form radiant with mild and heavenly lustre stood at one side of the ghostly throng, and they whose sufferings were mitigated turned anxiously towards him; but the others hid their faces in despair, and their low groanings fell upon my ear and chilled my heart.

"Then I heard again the low sweet solemn sounds from above, and these words reached me—

'*Venite ad me omnes qui laboratis et onerati estis, et ego reficiam vos. Alleluja.*'

"As they heard the sounds, the spirits that looked upon the angel moved towards him, and the light of his countenance fell upon them and bathed them with its illumination, and they grew whiter and purer in its radiance, and the trouble of their faces was lightened. And now I turned my eyes towards the wretched ones afar off, and, lo! a form, tall as a giant and black as a wintry tempest, stood beyond them, and the wail of their anguish swelled upon the air when they looked upon him. Then one amongst them cried aloud, with an exceeding bitter cry. But a voice, mild yet stern, said unto him—

"'As yet there is no remission for thee. Thou didst enjoy thy sin to the last. Thou tookest the unwary in thy snare, and despoiled the orphan and the innocent of his heritage. The accursed love of gold held thee to the last, and thou didst die with the patrimony of another in thy gripe!"

"Then the wretched spectre said, 'Who accuseth me?' Thereupon forth stood a form from out the crowd, and I knew it to be that of him who had brought me thither over the plain and the mountain. And he said—

"'I accuse thee. The wrongs and sorrows of my child will not let me rest in the grave. Restore that whereof thou hast robbed him.'

"Then said the angel,

"'Prefer thy charge.'

"And the spirit said,

"'With false dice did he win my fair lands; he brought me to an untimely death, and my heir to ruin.'

"And the other was silent, and denied not the accusation. Then said the angel to the accusing spirit,

"'Thy punishment is just; thy soul was covetous, and thou hast reaped the fruits of thy sin.'

"And the other answered,

"'I am justly punished, let me suffer; but my child'—

"A shade of ineffable commiseration passed over the bright countenance of the angel, and he said,

"'Mighty is the power of love! Thy prayer shall prevail for thy child. Let him restore that which he hath taken by fraud.'

"Then the dark and gigantic form stepped forward and said,

"'It may not be. The heritage has been made over by his own deed: he may not revoke it.'

"But the other said, sternly,

"'Thy power goeth not thus far, nor shalt thou countervail the decrees of mercy. Where is the deed?'

"Again the dark one spoke,

"'Thou canst not recall the past. Who shall say that the issue would not have been the same had there been no treacherous dealing? He sought a gambler's chance and wrought a gambler's sin. Shall he not abide a gambler's fate? Is he innocent because the other is more guilty? I appeal to thy own laws of justice!'

"'Thou hast appealed to justice,' said the angel. 'Be it so. Let time roll back.'

"In a moment the whole scene vanished from my sight, as the magic vision in a wizard's mirror, and I was in darkness."

"After a time a pale light shone near me, and I perceived it streamed from a lamp. The rays revealed to me a large and richly furnished room, with a table in the midst, whereon stood an antique candelabrum. At the table were seated two men, one of whom I recognised as the Cavalier of the Castel Vecchio; the other was the form of him whom he had accused. They were engaged in play, and dice lay before them. The Count took up the dice, and as he looked at them in the light of the lamp he saw that they were loaded, and he cast them away and demanded others. Then one whom I had not seen before, a fair youth, gave him other dice. And the two men played, and the Count lost the first game. Then they played again, and the Count won, and so they were equal. There was a pause of a moment, and a pang of agony made the face of the Count grow pale, and his lip quivered. He sighed deeply, and said, in a low stifled voice,

"'My son, my son!'

"But the brow of the other grew black, and he said impetuously,

"'Proceed with the game. Thou canst not question the result. I will abide by it.'

"Then they played again, and the adversary of the Count threw the highest on the dice, and a smile of triumph lit up his dark eye as the other took them up. I watched with my whole soul intent upon the issue. He threw, and his throw was as high as that against him. One chance more remained, and each threw in turn, and the Count uttered a cry of joy. He had won! There was a moment of silence, after which I heard a voice saying,

"'Bring forth the deed.'

"The fair youth came forward to the table, and laid upon it a parchment and materials for writing. Then the voice said to him who had lost,

"'Thou hast had justice even according to what man calls justice. Tear off the seal and the handwriting of him thou hast defrauded.'

"Then the form, slowly and reluctantly, as if forced by a power he could not resist, arose from his seat, and tore off a portion of the parchment, and the fair youth took it and held it in the flames of the lamp until it was consumed. Again I heard the voice saying to the same form,

"'Write now on the back of the parchment that thou dost release and annul the claim that thou didst gain by fraud.'

"The form took the pen and wrote as he was commanded. When it was done the voice said,

"'Now, sign thy name thereto.'

"Mutely and slowly the form obeyed, and suddenly a gust of wind swept through the chamber. The flame of the lamp rose up in the air, and all was darkness. The storm caught me up as it were upon its wings. I heard the thundering sound of hoofs, as I was borne with the speed of the whirlwind through the night air, and the next moment I found myself in the chamber in the Castle upon the black steed, in the self-same spot, where I mounted him. I felt him pant and tremble beneath me, and, rearing wildly up, he fell back upon me to the ground. How long I lay insensible, I know not, but when I opened my eyes, the broad light of day streamed through the large window upon me as I lay beneath the picture of the mounted cavalier, which had fallen from the panel where it hung the night before. I extricated myself from beneath the weight of the ponderous picture frame, and, when I stood upright, my brain reeled, I felt chill and dizzy, and my limbs ached, as if I had undergone violent and fatiguing exercise.

"Again I flung myself on the bed, and, despite the thoughts that passed confusedly through my mind, I soon sank into deep and dreamless sleep."

CHAPTER V.

THE CONSULTATION.

"THE creaking of the chamber door awoke me, and when I opened my eyes, the young Count of Castel Vecchio stood at my bedside.

"'*Caro amico*,' said my friend 'I fear I have broken in upon your slumber. I came to learn how you have slept during the wild and blustry night. The wind has been howling through the old castle, as though it mourned the departure of its old inhabitants. Ah! what is this I see?—my father's picture fallen from its place. This is, indeed, an ill omen; but omens now cannot affect me. It seems he, too, warns me that we can stay here no longer.'

"'This, then, is your father's portrait, dear Ferdinand,' said I. 'How strange!'

"'What is strange?' said the Count,

"'Do not ask me at present,' said I. I will rise now and join you presently in the *salon*.'

"'What! in your clothes still, Henri,' cried the Count in surprise, seeing me full dressed as I arose. 'Is it possible that you lay thus through the night? I fear you have slept but uncomfortably.'

"'It is true, Ferdinand, that I did not undress,' I replied, evading an answer to his last observation; 'but you know of old that I am a genuine traveller, and care not about such things.'

"My friend left me, and I arranged myself without delay. While I bathed my hot and aching brows with cold water, I reviewed the extraordinary scenes of the past night. All was clear, distinct and vivid before my mind, as palpable as any events of my life. I tried to believe it was but a dream, but dream never wore such reality as all that I now looked back upon. And, then, there was the picture to stamp all with the certainty of truth. I raised the heavy frame and set it upright; I looked at it with the expectation that the noble form of the old Count would again address me: but no, the lips were close and mute; and yet, I thought— nay I almost felt—that the keen black eye looked into my very soul, and commanded me to work out the mission of the past night, while the coal-black steed stood out from the canvas as if instinct with energy, and the veins of the head and limbs seemed as if swollen with recent and violent exertion. I hurried to the *salon*, and met my friend, and found him busied in preparations for travelling.

"'This is but scant courtesy for my friend,' said

he, with a melancholy smile, 'to constrain him to leave the roof so soon, which he has come so far to visit. But I am no longer its master.'

"'You will accompany me, dear Henri, to Messina. To-morrow I sail thence for Italy.'

"'Dear Ferdinand,' I replied, with emotion, 'I will not leave you, be your fate what it may. Whether you depart hence, or stay, myself, my fortune, my life are yours.'

"'A thousand thanks, dear Henri,' said the Count. 'Your friendship I prize dearly—dearer than ever, more I need not say. But why do you speak of staying here? The Marchése comes here at noon by appointment, to receive what I have no longer the right by law to retain. The moment I surrender the keys of the old castle, I leave it for ever.'

"A pang of manly grief shook his frame, and he sank on a chair and hid his face in his hands.

"I reverenced his grief, and was silent. I felt the language of common-place commiseration would be an insult to his sorrow, and I refrained. In a few moments he recovered his tranquillity, and rose up erect and firm. His eye shone with a proud and almost haughty lustre, and brought forcibly to my mind that of the old Count, as I had seen it in the picture.

"'Pardon me this weakness, Henri. It is the

first that you or any man has witnessed, and I trust shall be the last. I am not one to give way to despair. Have I not youth, and health, and strength, a strong heart and a clear conscience? Why then should I not hope? And now to our meal, for there is much to be done ere noon, and I feel that heaven has kindly sent you to aid and sustain me.'

"'Most truly do I believe so,' said I; 'and I cannot help expecting a happier issue of these trials than you hope for. My arrival at such a critical time looks something more than casual.'

"An incredulous and melancholy smile passed over the features of the Count, and the subject dropped. During breakfast, we conversed on indifferent topics, and each detailed what had occurred since our separation.

"When the repast was ended, I said to my friend,

"'Were you acquainted with the late Marchèse?'

"'Not at all. He spent much of his time in Italy, and only returned to the neighbourhood of Messina after my departure from this island.'

"'What character did he bear?'

"'Indifferent enough, I believe. In early life he was a man of dissolute and prodigal habits, and wasted a noble patrimony. In later years he became, as is not uncommon with such persons, penurious and avaricious in the extreme, and ere he died it is said that he more than restored his ruined fortunes.'

"'And his son?'

"'I have scarcely ever seen him, but I believe he has a fair reputation. His father and he had, they say, but little intercourse, and the son was in Germany when the old Marchèse died.'

"'Good. Tell me now, Ferdinand, did your father never communicate to any one the circumstances under which he transferred this property to the Marchèse?'

"'Never, that I could learn. Save servants there were none to whom he could do so, and he was not a man who confided in those below his own station. I was absent when he lost his estate, as I told you, and only became aware of the fact after his death.'

"'Did you see the deed?'

"'Certainly, and inspected it narrowly. I must do the young Marchèse the justice to say that he frankly afforded me every facility: but he had no information to give, beyond the fact of the instrument, which, he said, he found amongst his father's papers after his death.'

"'Well, Ferdinand,' said I, 'I cannot help entertaining a strong conviction that the old Marchese did not fairly come by the deed. You say the property was won at gaming?'

"'So it would appear, from the latest document I have found in my father's handwriting.'

"'And I firmly believe,' I rejoined, 'that the Marchese won by foul play. There are such things as false dice.'

"My friend started, and for a moment remained in thoughtful silence; at length he said—

"'Something I heard of this Marchese I now remember, which would almost lead me to think your suspicion may not be ill-founded. There was a report that he left Rome suddenly, in consequence of an affair with the Prince de B——, in which his character suffered.'

"'Now, listen to me, Ferdinand,' said I. 'Sit down quietly beside me,'—he was walking hurriedly up and down the room—'for I have much to tell. I pledge my existence and my honor as a gentleman that the Marchese cheated your father with false dice. May Heaven enable me to establish this fact as surely as I believe it!'

"I then related to him my strange adventures of the past night. He listened to me with profound attention to the end.

"'*Santissima Maria! che maraviglia!*' at last he ejaculated. 'Be it a dream, or vision, or reality, I believe it has figured forth the truth. Who shall say, Henri, how soul may communicate with soul?—how the spirits of the departed may visit us, even in these latter days, for important purposes, as we know they did in times of old?—how the spirit of the living may wander forth from the body when it lies buried in a sleep that is the similitude of death? I have myself seen, in Vienna, things too wonderful almost for credence, but that I was constrained not to disbelieve. But how are we to turn to account this supernatural revelation?'

"'Nay, you must leave that to me. I have not been made the instrument of this spiritual communication to no purpose. I shall persevere in working it out. Leave me for a space to my own reflections, while you proceed with other matters.'

"'Be it so, my friend,' said the Count. 'At all events, I know the worst that can happen, and I am prepared for it.'

"'*Coraggio!* my friend,' said I, rising from my seat, and pointing to the motto beneath his armorial bearings, that were blazoned over the mantelpiece, I added, '*A Dio mi fido:* forget not the trust of your ancestors.'

"I passed out through the oriel window that opened on a terrace facing the north-east. The day was serene, though dark and somewhat warm, and the wind, that had been high through the night, was now sunk to a calm. Dark masses of clouds still hung in the heavens, but blue streaks of ether broke through them here and there cheerily.

"As I surveyed the rich fields, over which the cattle were peacefully browsing, the dark forests of pine, oak, and beech, the growth of centuries, and caught the gleam of placid streams straying through the verdant plains, I felt as if they were endued with a voice that said to me—we shall not pass away from the race that has lived and died amongst us. I strode to the northward angle of the gravelled platform, and my eye caught the whole southern ascent of Monte Gibello. There it was, such as I had witnessed in my mystical transit—its base smiling in rich verdure, the pomegranate, and lemon, and orange, the trailing vine hanging in its graceful festoons; above these, the dense dark forests, the gloomy ravines, the lava torrents, like ribs bared by fire; and, higher still, the cone of smooth ashes surmounted by the crater, puffing forth its hot and smoky breath into the sky. While I marked all these, for the first time, they seemed to me as familiar as if I had trodden them a hundred times, and I felt the reality of all that I had gone through. I was aroused from my contemplations by the sound of horses moving rapidly, and the roll of wheels on the shingles.

"This ceased suddenly, and the clang of a bell smote startlingly on my ear. In a moment after, the wheels again rolled more slowly along the pavement. I looked at my watch, and, finding it was just noon, I re-entered the apartment where I had left the Count of Castel Vecchio."

CHAPTER VI.

THE POINT OF HONOR.

"When I again stood within the *salon*, I perceived the Count standing beside the tall mantelpiece that surmounted the antique fire-place. He held in his hands a large panel of dark oak, on which he was gazing with a contemplation so profound that he did not notice my approach, nor the sounds that had caused my return. As I drew near him, I found that the object which absorbed him was the portion of the woodwork on which the armorial bearings to which I have already referred were painted: he had, no doubt, separated from the surrounding timber in which it had been inserted, and torn down this, the last record of his ancestry; a solemn divesting of his name and pedigree from the pile that had for ages recognised his race as its owners. I laid my hand gently on his shoulder, and he turned his face towards me, with a smile, proud, yet melancholy.

"'It was the last tie that bound me to the old castle,' said he, 'and it's now severed. Henceforth, I am but a stranger.'

"'It was not well done, Ferdinand,' I answered reproachfully. 'Have you, then, disavowed your faith in that trust upon which your forefathers relied? With the assistance of that God in whom they trusted, you shall yet see it restored to its place.'

"At this moment, the old servitor entered, and, with a dejected voice, full of the most respectful sympathy, said, 'The Marchèse di N—— is without, Sir, and desires to know if it be your pleasure to receive him?'

"The Count started slightly, and his face grew pale as death, but his eye was bright, and almost stern, as he replied, composedly,

"'Conduct the Marchèse within, without delay. Say I await him.'

"In a short time the servant re-appeared, ushering in the Marchèse, and then retired, closing the door after him. The Count stepped forward a few paces, and inclined his head with a cold and formal salutation. The Marchèse bowed profoundly, and with deep respect. It was a touching sight to see the young noble, landless and houseless, standing in the midst of the room in his desolation and ruin, with his household gods prostrated around him; the apartment cheerless and in disarray, partaking, as it were, of the wretchedness of this, the last of its ancestral line. If aught on the part of the Marchèse could have aggravated the distress of the Count's position, there was nothing in his deportment to do so.

"'Conte del Castel Vecchio,' said he, 'I have come here by your own appointment. If your preparations be not complete, I shall most willingly depart, and await your perfect convenience.'

"'By no means, Sir,' said the Count, proudly, 'the Marchèse commands here, and I am ready to do what remains to be done. My arrangements are all made. My friend,' pointing to me, 'will assist me in this business.'

"The Marchèse turned towards me with a courteous inclination. For the first time, I looked attentively at his face, and was struck with the feeling that it was in some way not entirely unknown to me. The resemblance to him whom I had seen engaged at play with the old Count was too striking to be mistaken.

"'I am acquainted with the circumstances under which your lordship is here,' said I, addressing him; 'may I ask to see the deed by which you claim?'

"'Assuredly,' said he; 'it is but reasonable. I have brought it with me.'

"The Marchèse drew from the pocket of his travelling coat a small box, and, opening the lock with a gold key attached to his watch chain, took out a folded parchment. We approached the table, and he unfolded the document. It had the appearance of a deed drawn in the usual formal manner. I commenced to peruse it, and found it stated that Antonio Carlo, Conte del Castel Vecchio, was indebted to Giambattista, Marchèse di N———, in a large sum of money, which was specified; and that the former, in order to discharge the debt, thereby conveyed to the latter the Countship of Castel Vecchio, in the Piano di Catania and kingdom of Sicily, with the castle, and all the signorial rights and privileges annexed to it. The description of the lands, and the technicalities of the legal phraseology made up the rest of the writing. When I had arrived towards the end, I turned back the last fold, upon which the seals and signatures of the parties to the contract are to be found. The Count and the Marquis stood each at a different side of me, and opposite the one to the other. Both started as if struck with a bolt of thunder, and gazed at each other in silence. Neither seal nor signature was attached to the deed. A portion of 'the parchment had been manifestly removed, and, as it would seem, burned off, for the edge was irregular in its outline, and had a black, shrunk, charred appearance. The Marchése seized the deed, and inspected it with the most minute scrutiny; then laid it again on the table.

"'Sir Count,' said he, 'here is something which I cannot understand. Since last I produced this document for your satisfaction it has never been taken from this box, to my knowledge; the key I always carry about my person, and the Paris lock would defy the most skilful mechanist in Sicily. There is no trace of tampering,' he observed, looking narrowly at the lock and hinges; 'and yet there must have been some treachery. Speak, Conte del Castel Vecchio, can you throw light on it?'

"The Count's eye lit up fiercely, and a hot flush of indignation mounted to his brow.

"'Does your lordship dare to couple my name with such a word as treachery? You shall learn that I have not lost my honour with my lands.'

"The Marchèse was about to reply, when I interposed:

"'Gentlemen, let me entreat you both to be tranquil. This is a matter of business, and not to be discussed in hot blood and angry recriminations.'

"'I appeal to the honor of the Count,' said the Marchèse, 'which I believe to be above suspicion. Were not your father's signature and the seal of the Counts of Castel Vecchio attached to this parchment when last you saw it?'

"The Count was on the point of replying, but I promptly prevented him.

"'However that may be,' said I, 'the Count is not called on to answer your question. You come hither claiming his estates, upon the allegation of a legal conveyance of them. It is for you to establish that claim.'

"'Nay, nay, Henri,' said the Count, waving his hand impatiently, 'I shall never stand on such a pitiful defence. My Lord Marchèse has appealed to my honour, and shall not do so in vain. It is true, as he says, my father's hand and seal were both to the document when I saw it. How it is that they are not there now is as unknown to me as to the Marquis.'

"'Count,' said the latter, 'I expected no less from you; and I entirely believe what you have asserted.'

"'I decline to avail myself of the present condition of this instrument,' said the Count, firmly. 'Let us proceed as if it were as perfect as it was on the day I saw it.'

"The Marchése looked at the Count for a moment in silence. There was less of wonder than admiration and deep respect in his look. Contradictory feelings seemed struggling in his mind as he looked from the parchment to the Count, and from the latter to the parchment again. At length he said, slowly, and with some hesitation:

"'Count of Castel Vecchio, I have a proposition to make for your consideration and that of your friend. If you will now pay me one-half of the debt, for the discharge of which your father sold these estates to mine, I shall re-convey them to you; or, should you not be prepared to do so at present, I shall be ready to abide by the same arrangement at any time within twelve months, upon your paying me the sum I have mentioned, with interest.'

"'I thank you, my lord,' said the Count, in a softened voice. 'I am not insensible to the generosity of your offer, though I may not accept it. Your right, whatever it be, goes to the entire.'

"'Permit me,' said I, addressing the two nobles, 'to lay before you my views of this matter. Let me, too, entreat your lordship to bear with me, if, in so doing, I shall say anything which may surprise or displease you; and believe that I entertain the high respect for you which your conduct to-day entitles you to.'

"The Marquis silently bowed in acknowledgment, and I proceeded:

"'It is now plain that, on legal grounds, the Marchèse di N—— cannot establish a right to the territory of Castel Vecchio.'

"I looked at each as I said this. Neither of them ventured to dissent from my statement.

"'Well, then,' I continued, 'the transaction rests entirely upon the laws of honour between two men, who, I am convinced, hold those laws to be of the most binding obligation. The contract which the Count feels he is bound to ratify, the Marchèse believes he is justified in honour to enforce. Is it not so?'

"Each, in silence, bowed his assent.

"'You have heard, then, my lord, that the debt due by the Count's father to your's was contracted in gambling?'

"'I have heard so from the Count himself. Otherwise, I know nothing of the circumstances, save from the deed itself.'

"'That it was of the nature I mention, your lordship shall soon have proof. Be so good,' I continued, addressing the Count, 'to show his lordship the note which I read last night.'

"The Count took from the escritoire a folded paper, which I opened and read aloud:—

"'*To my son. Ruined, and by your father's madness. The patrimony of your ancestors will never be yours. In a moment of desperation, I played with the Marquis di N———. Alas! his good fortune never wavers, and I lost! Lost all—lands and house! I feel that I shall not live to hear your reproaches. You will accord forgiveness and prayers to the dead.—C. A.*'

"I handed the note to the Marchése.

"'I cannot doubt what you assert,' said he. 'Still, upon the principles of honour to which you have referred, and by which we are both disposed to abide, it is a debt as binding as any other.'

"'Undoubtedly, my lord: if honourably and fairly won.'

"The Marquis started, and coloured with displeasure.

"'Remember your promise to be patient,' said I,

'and hear me out. I believe, and I solemnly assert, that the Marchese di N———, your father, did not fairly win from the father of my friend.'

"'How, Sir,' commenced the Marchese, in rising indignation; 'do you mean to ——?' With a strong effort, he controlled his feelings, and continued more calmly: 'Proceed, Sir; let us have the proofs of your assertion.'

"'I have proofs, my lord,' said I, 'which to my own soul have brought conviction the most solemn and irresistible. How far you may deem them as cogent, I know not.'

"'Of that I shall judge,' replied the other, 'when I shall have heard them.'

"I own I felt much unwillingness to detail the strange incidents, which I have already mentioned, to the Marchese. Not only might he receive the narrative with utter disbelief, as an idle dream, but be disposed, perhaps, to view it as a dishonest attempt to impose on the well-known credulity of his countrymen in relation to supernatural things; and, besides, there was much, no matter in what light he might view the tale, which was calculated to offend him deeply, in reference to the memory and conduct of his father. While I thus hesitated, the scenes of the night passed again in review before me, when suddenly I remembered what, strange to say, had somehow escaped from my recollection, I mean the release which the form in the vision was forced to endorse on the cancelled deed. In a moment, I took the parchment, and turning the back of the last skin, I saw some writing endorsed upon it, to which was attached the name and seal of the late Marquis.

"'There is something here,' said I, 'which may supersede the necessity of my entering into further proof. Listen.' And I read as follows:—'*I, Giambattista di N———, do hereby acknowledge and declare that the sum in this deed stated as due to me by the Conte del Castel Vecchio was neither a lawful, just, or honourable debt, and that the conveyance of the estates herein is without consideration. I do, therefore, hereby annul and make void this deed, and, in sign thereof, have taken off the seal and signature of the said Count thereto, and I enjoin on my heir to cancel this instrument.*'

"To this was affixed the signature and seal of the late Marquis of N———.

"It would be quite impossible to convey an adequate idea of the surprise and horror depicted in the countenance of the Marchèse, as I read the foregoing. When I had ended, he reached forth his hand, took up the parchment, and examined every word and character of the endorsement. He then slowly replaced it upon the table. After a long and thoughtful pause, he said:

"'This is more mysterious and unaccountable than the disappearance of the seal. If it were here when last I saw the deed, it could scarcely have escaped my notice. The handwriting is surely that of my father, and,—merciful Heaven! can it be?—it bears date, "The Feast of All Souls, 18—." Even this very day. Either the hand of God or the machinations of the devil are in this matter.'

"'The latter it can scarcely be,' I observed; 'when we consider all the circumstances of the case.'

"'I know not,' said the Marquis. 'I can see no clue to this mystery. You said, Sir, you had proofs of ——' the young man hesitated, from a natural horror of pronouncing his father's name, coupled with false play—'proofs, I mean, of the circumstances under which the late Count lost at play with my father. I entreat you to let me hear them.'

"I felt that, after what had already occurred, I could not now refuse to put the Marquis in possession of the revelations made to me. I accordingly replied:

"'As it is your wish, my lord, I shall not withhold from you my reasons for believing that, as the writing acknowledges, the debt was neither a lawful, just, or honourable one.'

"I then made the Marquis acquainted with all of which I had previously informed the Count. When I reached the part that related to his unhappy father, he became profoundly agitated, and, sinking in his chair, he buried his face in his hands. When I ended, the Marquis arose. His countenance was pale, and as if full of humiliating shame, and traces of tears were in his eyes. He took the deed in his hand, and, bearing it to the fire, cast it upon the smouldering logs of firewood, and watched till it was slowly consumed. Neither myself nor the Count interrupted him by word or movement. There was that about him, and in the manner in which he addressed himself to the work he had to do, which commanded our reverence, and forbade us to check him. When the parchment was a shrivelled and shapeless mass, he heaved a deep sigh, that spoke less of regret than of a relieved spirit, and, turning to my friend, said:

"'I have obeyed the injunction of the dead, and have destroyed all evidence of claim to your property. I rejoice that my soul has not to bear the weight of despoiling you, however unwittingly, of that to which I have no just right. I will now leave you, Count of Castel Vecchio. May you be happy in your ancestral possessions. But, ere I go, let me have the consolation of knowing that you acquit me of all knowledge of the means by which this false claim was acquired. I could not bear to be thought lowly of by one whom I have learned to respect so highly.'

"'Marquis,' cried my friend, deeply moved, 'I do acquit you from my soul. Suffer me to embrace you as a friend from henceforth.'

"The Count held out his hand, which the other grasped in silence; but I could see that his frame shook with the violence of the varied emotions that agitated him. A few hours after, the Marquis took his departure. The young men took leave of each other with a mutually cordial respect, and assurances of meeting again.

"Ferdinand, too, left the Castle that evening, and I accompanied him; but he did not go as an outcast from the home of his forefathers, never to revisit it. On the contrary, full of hope, he departed for Italy, to communicate the strange and sudden change in his fortunes to her for whose sake he chiefly prized them. Ere we left the house, I took upon myself two tasks—one was, to see the picture of the old mounted cavalier safely and securely suspended from the wall of the sleeping apartment whence it had fallen; the other I performed with my own hands, replacing in the wainscot, over the mantelpiece in the *salon*, the armorial bearings of the Counts of Castel Vecchio. When I had done so, I led Ferdinand into the room, just as we were about departing. We both stood before the tablet; and, as I repeated solemnly to him the pious motto of his race, '*A Dio mi fido*,' he raised his hat reverently from his brow, bowed low his bared head in silent thankfulness to Him whose name I uttered, and then threw himself, sobbing, into my arms. Oh! how fully I understood the happiness of that moment!"

CHAPTER VII.

SUNSHINE AFTER STORM.

"TIME passed on, as he passes ever. *Time*, the unchangeable, the inexorable, the constant; and yet, who seems to each one who views him so diverse in his nature and appearance. To some, he comes dancing along with the springy step of youth, crowned with flowers, and led onward with the song and the dance. For others, he rushes wild, turbid, and rapid as the torrent swollen with the rains of winter; like it, too, sweeping away bank and barrier, and the fair smiling prospects that the husbandman has prepared with all his providence for summer.

Upon some, how stealthily he creeps! they hear not his step and they mark not his progress till they find he has been with them, passing over some sweet spot of their heart's garden; leaving the marks of his feet upon its verdure, and of his scythe amongst its flowers. And, oh! there are those who measure anxiously the journey he has to make to some distant point—the goal of some crowning happiness, or the respite from some life-consuming sorrow—the moment when they shall lay aside their heavy burden, and lie down wearied to take their long, dreamless slumber. Still, for each and for all of these, he is the same in reality. As lusty and as strong as the day he first issued forth from eternity upon his mighty journey, his pace is ever unchanging; he knows no hurry, no loitering, no turning backwards, or aside; but onward, onward ever, pressing with resistless purpose towards the shadowy precincts of that eternity which is once more to receive him.

"Time passed on, and I again found myself travelling from Catania along the road that led to Castel Vecchio. It was spring—that season the loveliest of the year; all the brighter for the gloom of winter, now passed and gone; full of the vivifying influences of renascent life in all living things. The tender green was on the corn and the grass, the herb and the tree were bursting and filling with the bud and the young green leaf. The earth was vocal with the chirping of the cicada and the hum of the toiling bee, as he plunged deep in the bells of the flowers, or sipped the sweet out of the fragrant thyme; the heavens rang with the warblings of innumerable birds, while the sportive squirrels sprang from tree to tree. It was near evening, and I threw myself back in my calash, to enjoy the pleasurable sense of nature's loveliness. I turned my eyes from the charms of the earth, and looked eastward along the beautiful and tranquil sea. It stretched far away, tideless and calm, and glowing beneath the radiance of the setting sun; while, skirting along the low line of the horizon, the clouds that were dim a few hours ago now caught the sun's rays, which touched them with the true power of the fabled Midas, and turned them into gold—or, rather, into a ruddy hue such as we see taken by burnished copper.

As I watched these brilliant tints, they brought forcibly to mind how wonderfully the workings of God's moral providence are typified in the natural world; how hope and happiness grow out of despair and sorrow, even as the golden panoply of evening is the child of the cloud and the vapour lit up by the sunshine.

"I remembered my last visit to the Castle: ah! how different were the circumstances under which I now returned. I had but yesterday left my dear friend Ferdinand at Naples, after witnessing his espousal to the lovely and faithful girl whose heart had still clung to him, through weal and through woe, and I now hurried on before them, to see that the old castle was in readiness, with its brightest face, to receive the Count and his bride. Again I drove up to the ancient gateway, and my postilion rang at the ponderous oaken door; but the summons was now answered with alacrity, and cheery faces met me in anxious expectation. I passed into the house, and had to answer many a kindly inquiry about the Count and Countess, and heard on every side hopes expressed of their speedy return. After I had given such orders as I thought necessary for the reception of the Count, and partaken of the good cheer of my old acquaintance, the ancient servitor, I reclined in the bay-window of the *salon*, in pleasant rumination. At length, my old acquaintance entered, with two antique candelabra in his hand, and, setting them down on the table, said:

'Pardon, Eccelenza, I would wish to know in what apartment you will sleep to-night? I fear that in which you slept on your former visit was not comfortable.'

"'I should particularly desire to sleep in it again to-night,' said I.

"'As you please, Eccelenza,' said the man, and retired.

"That night I passed in the panelled chamber. The cavalier, on his black charger, was there just as I had left him, and the last object which my eye recognised, ere it closed in slumber, was that of the old Conte del Castel Vecchio. But my sleep was dreamless and pleasant, and I rose in the morning thoroughly refreshed, and with a buoyant and hopeful spirit. At noon I stood on the steps of the heavy gothic portico, as a gay travelling chariot, drawn by four spirited horses, dashed through the gateway and along the court-yard, and pulled up short and suddenly beside me. The Count was on the ground in a moment, and in my embrace. The next instant he turned quickly around, and tenderly gave his arm to the Countess, and led her within the porch. As he held a hand of each in his, he exclaimed,

"'Dearest Francesca, dear Henri, how happy am I with such a wife, and such a friend!'

"We were all moved, as the thoughts of the past, its perils, and its sorrows, at that moment involuntarily arose upon our memories, and we entered the house in silence. I shall not profane the sacred privacy of the domestic hearth, by recounting the happy evening which I passed with my friend and his bride. On the morrow, I felt that it would be well to leave them alone for the intercommunings of their own hearts, so I determined on a solitary ramble through the surrounding country. I mounted one of the Count's horses, and rode through the Piano di Catania, and thence to the foot of Mount Etna.

"Oh! how vividly was every step of the way painted on my memory—wood, and forest, and glade, the meadows, the pasture, and the villages: there were the lemon and orange trees, the vine and the pomegranate, the river, and the ravine, the lava flood and the cone of ashes. There was not a spot that was not familiar to me. When I had reached the summit of the mountain, the sun was just about to set. It was a glorious spectacle. North, lay the sea, cold and tranquil, spotted with its islands; while the southern coast of Italy lay to the north-east. Then the sea again, with its waves rippling along the coast of Sicily—while to the west, the eye stretched over the rich and undulating country that lay at the foot of

Monte Gibello. And there, above all, was the mountain itself, with the light vapoury clouds rising up from within it. All again passed like the scenes of a phantasmagoria before my spirit's sight, and I knew not which scene was the more real, that of the Feast of all Souls, or this of to-day. At night I rejoined my friends, and the next morning I was forced to leave them; but I left them in the possession of as much happiness as ordinarily falls to the lot of any in this changeful and uncertain life. Ere a year had passed over, I heard again from the Count. From him I learned that the Marchèse di N———, who had associated little with mankind since the period when I was first introduced to him, had died suddenly a short time since, leaving by his will his estates, one-half to the Count del Castel Vecchio, and the other half to be applied in masses for the repose of the soul of his father. The latter injunction was most religiously obeyed, and a solemn service was thenceforth to be performed for the repose of the soul of Giambattista, Marchèse di N———, at the chapel of St. ———, in Naples, on every FEAST OF ALL SOULS."

CHAPTER VIII.

A REVELATION.

WHEN our companion had ended his story, no one for a time seemed disposed to break the silence that ensued. The lights burned dimly in the earthen lamps, which stood on the table, and now sent up a dry, thin, feeble flame, that showed the oil was well-nigh exhausted.

The logs, too, in the large fire-place, smouldered in their white ashes, and the shadows in the recesses of the large unfurnished room assumed strange and fantastic shapes, that well accorded with the impressions so wild a narrative were calculated to leave on the imagination. The old gentleman was the first to break the spell, which he did in a low tone, half grumble, half soliloquy, in which the words, "hallucination, fantasy, nightmare, casual coincidence," were alone audible. His daughter seemed more deeply affected, and, I could plainly see, she was very nervously excited.

"Dear me," said the girl, her blue eyes glancing furtively around, "what a wonderful adventure! Had I seen such things, I do not think I should have ever enjoyed an easy hour afterwards."

"Fudge!" said her father, almost angrily.

"What is your opinion, Mr. ——?" addressing himself to me.

"My opinion is," I replied, "that the gentleman who has seen all these wonders which he has narrated is entitled to enjoy his own experiences: I cannot controvert them."

Pierre, as seemed to be his habit, said nothing, but, emerging from his nook in the ample chimney, he knocked the ashes out of his pipe, and, coming over to the table, raised the wick in one of the little earthen lamps, and signing to his master, in a manner at once respectful and peremptory, the latter arose from his seat, and wishing us a courteous good-night, followed his servant from the room.

By this time it was far advanced in the night. The old gentleman and his daughter discussed the comparative advantages of retiring to their bed-rooms, or sitting out the remaining hours of darkness where they were. The young lady's fears pleaded strongly in favor of the latter, and it was so decided accordingly. Thereupon, I rose up, poked out a few more logs of firewood, which I threw on the fire, and having assisted in disposing of some cloaks and shawls, so as to make our fair companion as comfortable as circumstances would permit, I felt it my duty to depart, and leave the two alone. I ascended a few ricketty stairs to the garret assigned me. It was a miserable and cheerless room, in which, from numerous holes in the floor and skirting, the rats were accustomed to revel undisturbed. A wretched truckle bed lay in one corner, near to which stood the only chair which the room contained, and at the other end was a chest, on which were placed a basin and water-ewer.

I closed the door, but found to my dissatisfaction that there was no lock upon it. I took off my coat and boots, and lay down in the rest of my clothes, using the precaution of taking my pistols to bed with me. Despite of the gambols of the rats, which coursed about the room, I contrived to snatch a few hours of sleep, and was again in the kitchen shortly after daybreak. When I entered, the old gentleman and his daughter were already astir, and the latter was giving directions to the squalid and drowsy Hebe to procure some coffee. Pierre now entered, and I inquired for his master.

"He has had a restless night," said the man, "and is not yet risen."

"A very strange personage is your master," said the Englishman, rather bluntly. "Pray has he had many such adventures as that which he related last night?"

"*Ma foi*," said Pierre, "he may have had a thousand of the same sort. Who knows?"

"You are going to Rome," said I. "Whence do you come?"

"From Marseilles, Monsieur," replied the servant.

"And did your master really see all the awful things that he told us of last night?"

"*Le Dieu le sait*," said Pierre, with a shake of his head. "My master is a great author, a *notabilité* of Paris; and he has written so much, and dreamed so much in his day that he does not quite know what is reality and what is fiction," and Pierre touched his forehead significantly. "He has been ill of late, and his physicians have forbidden his writing for a time, and ordered him to the South of Italy, and his friends have begged of me to accompany him."

"Ah! what an interesting enthusiast," sighed the young lady.

"As mad as a March hare, by Jupiter," said the Englishman to me.

I bowed to each, but said nothing. Perhaps my own notions were not very different from the opinion of either.

Christmas Eve.

A TALE OF TWO TRAVELLERS.

CHAPTER I.

"GOD help the houseless and the wanderer this wild night!" said the parson.

"Amen, dear uncle!" answered Ruth.

There was nothing very striking either in the prayer or the response. Each might have been uttered by the lips of hundreds on that dark, dreary Christmas Eve. The man of wealth in his luxurious mansion, as he looked around his well-furnished room where every appliance ministered to his comfort, where close-curtained windows excluded the blast, and a blazing fire dispelled the bitter cold: he might have said, "God help the houseless!" and, having commended such to God's help, felt that he had done quite enough—what did they want more? "Depart in peace; be ye warmed and filled." And some of this world's poor children, some lone widow in her cheerless garret—a soul rich in grace, and poor in everything else—might have breathed the prayer with all the earnestness which her own sense of misery hallowed and intensified. And the ejaculation of the one would have fallen dead as it passed the lips, for it came from a dead heart; while the prayer of the other would have gone right up to the Father of the fatherless.

He who uttered the prayer belonged to neither class; but he uttered the words as one who felt all their significance, and spread them out before God: there was heartiness and devotion in his tone and manner.

As you looked at the man, you would have felt assured that he was one of those who, when he prays God to help, knows that He helps through His appointed means, and would have girded himself to the task of helping for God's sake—as God's fellow-labourer.

'Twas a wild night, the parson had said, and said truly. A hard frost had set in some days before, with a strong north-east wind, but in the afternoon the wind veered about a few points to the west; the heavens became filled with dull, leaden-hued clouds, and then down came the snow, in thick, blinding flakes, drifting with the gusts, and filling up dykes, and lying deep against fences, and covering the sprays and branches of the leafless trees with a strange unwonted foliage, that bowed them down as laden with an ungenial burden. Over the wide, waste common, upon the skirts of which stood the parsonage, a few perches in advance of the village of Ashton-le-Moors, was spread a white sheet of trackless snow, obliterating the traces of the roadway that traversed it, and leaving no landmark visible to guide the wayfarer. The pastor, indeed, had found it no easy task to make battle against the wind and snow-fall, as he pushed sturdily through the drift in the village street to his own homestead. The man had been out all day amongst his people, looking after their wants, distributing to their necessities, cheering, comforting, counselling; for he was not one of your parsons who preach and pray on Sundays, and leave the people to take care of themselves the rest of the week. No; he was an active, earnest fellow, robust in mind and body, who went to his Master's work with a will that would have done your heart good to see—one that everybody knew and loved, from the old crone in the almshouse to the chubby urchin that sailed rushboats in the millpond.

"God help the houseless! And now, dear Ruth, I think we may leave the poor fellow awhile to nature; a few hours' rest and sleep will restore him. See, he is quite calm, he slumbers as peacefully as a child. Come, get me something to eat, for I am as hungry as a wolf. And here, Sybil, take my overcoat, and shake the snow off it, and put it to dry."

Then he drew a chair to the fire, gave it a great, hearty poke, that made the coal flare up in a blaze, and crackle as if resenting the assault, and, stretching out his legs, fell into a reverie, till aroused by the entrance of the meal, to which, after a hearty thanksgiving to God, he addressed himself with the vigour of one who had earned an appetite by hard work.

While the parson is eating, and Ruth is smilingly helping him to the choicest bits, I may as well explain the scene with which I have opened. The short winter day had closed, and the darkness had set in. Ruth was anxiously awaiting the arrival of her uncle, when she heard a heavy step in the hall, the door of the room was flung open, and the stalwart figure of the good man appeared, staggering beneath a burden which he bore upon his back; while at his heels a huge Newfoundland dog toiled along, carrying a large pack that hung from his neck and swung beneath his fore-feet.

The man laid down his load gently before the fire.

"Here, Ruth, is a poor fellow I found on the common outside. But for Brave I should not have discovered him. The good dog smelt him at a distance, and drew me to him. He must have lost the road, and wandered aside till he fell into the snow-drift in the dyke. He was insensible, and would soon have perished had we not found him. So I strapped his pack to Brave, and heaved him upon my shoulders, and here we are. Now release Brave from his load—noble old fellow!" and he patted the dog on the head; "and get something to refresh us and tell old Sybil to fetch a couple of thick blankets, and we shall get the poor fellow about quickly."

And so they did—these three good, active, Christian people; they poured a few teaspoonfuls of brandy down his throat, and chafed his limbs at the fire, add after a little he came to himself, with a long, heavy sigh, and gazed wildly at the women. Then, uttering a groan, he fell back shudderingly, muttering, in a low, broken voice—

"Not yet! not yet! O merciful Lord! Surely I have not yet passed beyond the grave!"

The parson took from a shelf a small phial, and pouring a little of the narcotic from it into the man's mouth, it soon produced the desired effect, and he sank into a tranquil sleep. Then they lifted him up, laid him on the couch in the recess near the fireplace, drew over a large screen to shelter him from the draught and light, and, covering him up snugly, left him to his repose.

Now all this happened, let me tell my readers, before I or any of them was born—the better part of a century ago, in what they call the good old times. Good times they were in a sense, but not as good as times that followed, or as the times which will be, I trust, before long again. America had achieved her independence; the war with the French and Spanish was over, Rodney had swept them from the West Indian waters; and England was beginning to breathe again. But the people had not yet learned to know their rights or their power; they had but scant education, and no voice in the councils of the nation. The press was feeble and fettered, and its publications rarely made their way into the homes of the masses. The steam-engine and the spinning-jenny were only in their infancy; the power-loom was not invented. The mighty resources of commerce and manufactures were yet but as the dreams of the enthusiast. Manchester had just begun to export cotton fabrics, and all England imported but twenty millions of pounds of cotton in the year. Good times they were, in a sense, but thank God we have lived to see better, when England has become the mart for the world; her prosperity, material and moral, advanced; her people more civilised, more enlightened, more educated; and the streams of knowledge and of truth, flowing from a thousand printing presses, percolating through every vein and artery of her social system.

All this time the snow is falling, and the gusts of wind are driving it now and again patteringly against the window panes, where the parson is at his meal. When he had finished, he and Ruth drew their chairs pleasantly together, and he told her of his day's labours amongst his flock, and what Christmas cheer he had provided for the poor; and Ruth asked tenderly for the old man who had got the rheumatism, and the bed-ridden woman in the almshouse; and so they chatted till the evening was waning into night, and the parson said—

"Now, dear Ruth, leave me for an hour or two to myself, to prepare for to-morrow; but come back and kiss me before you go to rest. I mean to sit up to hear the merry bells chime in the Christmas morning."

"And so, too, shall I, uncle," said the girl; "and now I'll go to help old Sybil to deck her kitchen with holly, and to light the Christmas candle."

CHAPTER II.

WHEN Ruth had left the room the parson took down from a bookshelf a Bible—a thick quarto, covered with green baize—and laying it on the table before him, opened it for the purpose of his night's meditation. As he turned over the leaves, his eye was arrested by a page in which some verses were underscored with ink. He paused and read them. They were from that sublime psalm of thanksgiving in which David recounts the mercies and providence of God:—

"They that go down to the sea in ships, that do business in great waters;
"These see the works of the Lord, and his wonders in the deep."

And so he read on of the storm and wave that caused men's hearts to melt with trouble, till he came to the verse—

"Then are they glad because they be quiet; so he bringeth them unto their desired haven."

The man gazed long and lovingly upon these verses, and closing the book with a sigh, he threw himself back in his chair and closed his eyes. But the eyes of his spirit were not closed. They saw long-past scenes rise up, as in the dreams of a sick man, and stand out in solemn and sad memories. There was the old, familiar home of his mother; and there he stood, a young, brave boy, beside her, full of hope and spirit, and he remembered the blessing, as she gave him a parting kiss, and put that old Bible into his hands, and showed him the verses that she had marked for him. And now where is that mother? And where are all the hopes of his youth? And where is —— ? The man sprang up, half fiercely, as if indignant at the feeling that had over-mastered him. Then he cried, "Father, not my will but thine be done!" and he sank on his knees in prayer, to rise up again, in a brief space, calm, resigned, self-collected—the same strong-minded, earnest man, to bear and to work in this world of work and suffering. And so he again opened the old Bible, and he read, and from time to time made notes for his Christmas sermon for the simple folks of Ashton-le-Moors. And so he worked on, till a clanging of the bell at the gate, and the barking of Brave, broke upon his labour. Up he sprang, and hurried out. At the gate stood a figure covered with snow, who craved shelter from the storm.

"I have lost my way," said he; "and but that I saw the light from your window, I suppose I should have to put up with a bed in the snow to-night. Will you let me in?"

"Willingly, and glad you found your way here. Come in. Down, Brave! Down, I say, sir!"

And so they entered the house.

The parson assisted the stranger to divest himself of a large coat, and he stood revealed a strong, thick-set man in sailor's garb, with grizzled hair and weather-beaten face, having a deep blue scar across the brow over the right eye, like a sabre cut.

"A hard night, master," said he, as he held his numbed hands over the fire. "I've been out many a hard night on sea and land, but seldom a harder than this."

"So it is, friend. But you are now safely housed from the wind and snow without. Come, what say you to a cut of this cold meat and a flagon of ale?"

"I shan't say anything against it. I've trudged many a weary mile since I've tasted bit or sup; and a nor'-wester sharpens a man's appetite woundily."

The stranger fell upon the food ravenously, and after a vigorous and lengthened attack upon platter and cup, he pushed them aside at last with a sigh, as of one who had done his duty, and was thoroughly satisfied.

"Well, friend, might one ask where you come from. You seem a stranger in these parts."

"You say true; I was never in this country before. I left Portsmouth yesterday, and have travelled, to the best of my calculation, twenty miles to-day. I was making for Ashton-le-Moors, which they told me is on my road northward, when the snow-storm came on, and I lost my way. Is it far from this?"

"Not very. You have not gone much astray, after all, and might have fallen upon worse quarters."

"Ay, sir, truly; I am grateful for your kindness. A roof over one's head is more than many a one merits, if he got his deserts; to say nothing of a good meal and a warm fireside. How far may it be to Leighton-Super-Mare?"

"A good sixty miles, at the least—away on the eastern coast."

"Sixty miles!" repeated the man with a sigh; "so far? I thought to reach it to-morrow; but that can't be."

"Nay, good fellow; to-morrow is no day for wayfaring. You shall rest here on our holy Christmas

Day; you shall be one of my flock—a stray sheep that has wandered into my fold."

"You are a clergyman, sir?"

"Ay, and in my Master's name I bid you welcome."

"I am not much used to such kindness, sir," said the man, his voice betraying some emotion; "and somehow it overcomes me. I have seen a good deal of the rough of life, and but little of the smooth. Ah, sir! I have often longed to meet one to whom I could speak out my mind. I think the load would not be quite so heavy to bear if I could show it to another."

"In the name of God, whose minister, I am," said the pastor, solemnly, as he rose and laid his hand on the shoulder of his guest, "speak your grief to me, whatever it may be. With me it shall be a sacred trust; I may console, or, at all events, advise you. Out with it, man, in God's name, I say!"

"Listen, then," said the stranger; "it is neither a long nor a very eventful story, though a sad one."

And so he began.

CHAPTER III.

"I ASKED you, sir, just now, about Leighton-Super-Mare; belike you may have been there?"

"I have," said the pastor.

"Ah, then you will know the harbour and the quay, and the long street that runs straight up the hill, and the little square, with the church and the school-house and the parsonage. Ay, ay, I see them all before me as if it were but yesterday. Don't you remember them?"

The host waved his hand impatiently; then he placed his elbows on the table, and rested his forehead upon his palms, as one prepared to listen attentively.

The stranger continued—"Well, in that long street I was born, now well nigh forty years ago. Next door to us lived a family who had come from some distant part of England—I don't know where—a widow, whose name was Godwin, with her son John, and a little girl, an orphan (the child of a dead sister), and her nurse. My mother showed what kindness she could to the widow, whose appearance was much above her condition, for she seemed poor enough.

The young people of both families became intimate; John and I were sworn friends at school, and in our play hours Grace Towers was ever with us in our sports. A day scarcely ever passed that did not find us together—rambling, when the weather was fine, on the seashore, or along the downs; or, when the rain or the storm kept us within doors, telling stories, or reading tales of travels and adventures, in which John Godwin took great delight—little Grace listening, in hushed attention, with her large, serious black eyes gazing on the reader. Well, sir, time ran on. One day was like another, and we grew up to be more than boys and girl; but still the same in friendship, only that Grace somehow seemed to be more shy and restrained than of old, and the lads began to treat with more respect the child that was now growing and ripening into a lovely young woman—the loveliest in the town, or the country far and wide. At last the time came when John and I were done our schooling, and were to do something for ourselves in the world. My lot was chosen for me already; I was to help my father in his shop, and succeed him when he grew old. John's course was not so plain before him. His mother was growing feeble in her health, and her thin, pale face showed the working of an anxious mind upon her.

There were almost daily secret conferences between the mother and son. But I never knew what was the subject of them, for on this point only John withheld his confidence from me, and would not bear to be questioned; 'twas plain they were not always pleasant, for on one or two occasions, after such meetings, his eyes were red, and his manner sad and troubled. At last, out it all came one day. John was going to America, where, as I gathered from some expressions that fell from him, he had relatives. The plan did not please his mother, who at last gave her consent, sorely against her wishes; but the young man, though loving and dutiful, had a strong will, and a bold, hopeful heart, and was a stout, manly fellow; and he spoke of coming home again after a few years, prosperous and happy. The day before he was to leave home, John and I had a long walk after dayfall along the cliffs, and he opened his mind to me about his future plans, and he asked me to be watchful of those he was leaving behind him. And I promised that I would be as a son to his mother, and—and——"

The man stopped abruptly and passed his hand over his forehead, as if agitated by the remembrance of something painful. After a short time he recovered his composure, and resumed—

"When John was gone I kept the promise I gave him, to be as a son to his mother; God knows how truly. But somehow, she never was the same after he left her. She grew feebler in health and more depressed in spirits every day; and I saw too plainly that her life was not likely to be a long one. And so, too, did poor Grace, as she watched over her and cared for all her wants; oh, how tenderly! She, too, seemed as if a change had come over her nature. Light and gayhearted no longer, but calm, and thoughtful, and uncomplaining, she looked as if she had put years upon her of a sudden, and become a sober, saddened woman, going through every duty without failing, but without hope. Well, well, let me pass on!

"A little way outside the town there was an old manor house—a lonely place, with a large lawn all around it, and a straight avenue of beech-trees leading up to it. A rich farmer, of the name of Austin, lived in it, and rented the manor lands to which it was attached. He was lately dead, and his son Mark now occupied the place. We all knew him, but were not intimate, for he was a shy, distant young fellow, and we thought, proud of his wealth.

"Now and then he called in to see Mrs. Godwin, and, by degrees, his visits became more frequent, and he would bring the sick woman some little delicacy from the farm or the dairy. Time passed on. John Godwin was a year gone, and no letter ever came from him; but we heard that he had joined the American insurgents, and fallen in the first encounter with the British troops. After this intelligence his mother never held up her head, and sank fast.

"One day, when Grace had left the room where we sat, Mrs. Godwin told me that Mark Austin had asked Grace in marriage some time since, and that the girl had now consented to become his wife. The news came upon me like a clap of thunder. I then, for the first time, thoroughly understood the nature of my own feelings towards her; that I loved her too dearly to endure that she should ever be the wife of another. I concealed my grief and confusion as well as I could, and, at the earliest moment left the room, to seek a confirmation of my fears from Grace herself. I found her pale, calm and self-collected. To the question, which I could scarcely ask, she answered that it was true; she had accepted the proposal of Mark Austin. Then I lost all power over myself, and, in a passion of grief and despair, revealed to her all my love, and besought her not to cast off my long-tried affection for the love of one whom she could scarcely love in return. The girl gazed at me with a look of surprise and terror: then, bursting into tears, she said—

"'George, George! why do you tell me this, to add to my wretchedness? But I cannot retract; my hand is pledged, though I may have no heart to give with it.'

"Then she left me, and I saw her no more that day. I shall never forget the night that followed—a cold, dark night, with a drizzling rain. My brain was on fire; I could not rest within doors, and so I went out, down the dreary, plashy street, till I reached the quay. It looked desolate and deserted; no one was abroad, and I paced up and down, and thought over my new, great, terrible sorrow, till I felt half mad and reckless. I was roused by a step near me, and, looking up, I saw Mark Austin within an arm's length of me. I have often since vainly asked myself what brought him there that night. Was it the devil or fate, or the will of an angry God that sent him in my way to tempt me beyond what I was able to resist? I seized him by the arm, and poured out a torrent of wild remonstrances, and hate, and imprecations. I demanded how he dared come between me and my love. I accused him of stealing into an unprotected household, to rob it of its treasure. I told him he was a mean, unmanly fellow, to force a girl to marry him when she did not love him. Ay, she hated him, and loved another. And then, with an oath, I swore that he should give her up at the peril of his life or mine. My first words he bore with a quiet, contemptuous silence that enraged me. As I went on, his sluggish blood grew warmer; and as I finished, his passion seemed as high as my own. He flung me off with a curse, and called me liar. In a moment I sprang upon him, and we closed in a deadly struggle. At last he thrust his hand within my neckcloth, and twisted it tightly, till I gasped for breath. I felt almost strangled, the blood gushed up into my eyes, and in another moment I should have been choked. I released my right hand, with which I had clutched his hair, and drawing a clasp-knife from my pocket, I drove the blade down the left side of his neck. Instantly he loosed his hold, and, with a groan, fell over the edge of the quay down into the sea, which was then at low water. I heard the plash, and then I strained over the spot and tried to look into the darkness for the form below. I could see nothing, but I heard one deep groan, and no more—not a sound or a stir, though I listened for many minutes. Then I knew that he was dead, and I rushed away from the spot up the lonely street—a murderer, who could not even dare to reap the fruits of his guilty deed, or seek the love of her for whom I had incurred a murderer's doom. Hurrying home, I let myself in unperceived, collected what money I could lay hands on, tied up a few articles of clothes in a bundle, and fled away in the dark night from everything and everybody I cared for in the world. As the morning broke, I found myself entering the seaport town for which I was making, and before night I was enrolled as a seaman on board a ship of war, and was sailing away from my native land. I need not tell you, sir, what scenes I have passed through since that time; how I served in every part of the world; what battles I have been in, and how often I have periled my life as a thing not worth caring for, and how Death passed me by to strike down some one to whom life was sweet; how I fought under Sir Samuel Hood and the brave Rodney off the West India Islands, and was in the glorious fight off Martinique, when Rodney broke through the lines of the French fleet—ay, ay! I remember that day well, sir," continued the man, almost forgetting his sorrow for a moment, in the pride and exultation of a British seaman. "I was in the *Canada*—only a seventy-four—when we bore down gallantly upon the *Ville de Paris*—the flagship of the French admiral, the Count de Grasse, the largest man-of-war upon the seas; and we poured a broadside into her, and then another, till we shattered her to a wreck. But why should I talk of those things? what share had I in the glory? My hands were stained with blood, but it was not the blood of a foeman killed in lawful war, but the blood of a countryman murdered—murdered! And so, while others were rejoicing, I stole away from them, for I saw the face of the man I had killed ever before me in the midst of the merriment, and heard his groan when the cheering was the loudest. Since then I have spent my life upon the seas till I was paid off, a few days ago, at Portsmouth. Then a longing that I could not resist came upon me to see once more the place of my birth, and learn if any of those whom I loved are still living. And so, sir, I was making my way to the old town when the snow-storm overtook me. I know the risk I run, but something drives me forward, it may be, to expiate my crime. And yet I doubt if there is any one left who would recognise this scarred and weather-beaten hull; besides, there was no one present on that terrible night, and the dead cannot rise to testify against me."

"George Masters, *I* rise to testify against you—

to demand vengeance for the blood that you have shed."

The two men sprang to their feet, and turned to the spot whence these appalling words proceeded; and there, beside the screen, in the dim obscurity of the shaded light, stood the form of a man with pallid and emaciated features, on which the flicker of the fire cast a strange, spectral hue. The sailor stood rigid with terror, gazing on the apparition in speechless fascination. At length he said, speaking slowly, and with an effort—

"Has the grave given up its dead? Mark Austin, I adjure you, say, are you in the body or in the spirit?"

"George Masters, I am a living man."

"O God, I thank thee!" cried Masters, heaving a profound sigh, that seemed to dispel a weight from his heart.

"Aye, thank God; but no thanks to you, murderer in will, if not in work; in the eyes of God, if not in the eyes of man!"

"I sought to kill you in self-defence."

"Liar! who sought the occasion?"

"It is true; it is true! Forgive, as God has been merciful to you."

"Listen, you that would have taken my life, and

you, worthy sir, that have saved it, listen to my story, as I have listened to that which has been told."

And the man sat down and began to clear up the mystery.

CHAPTER IV.

"GEORGE MASTERS, when you struck at the life of the man that never knowingly wronged you, and I fell into the water, I thought, as you did, that I had received my death blow. The water was then low—as low as five feet—enough to break my fall, but not to drown me. I rose to the surface, and found I could stand with my head out of water. The knife had glanced aside, and gave me but a long flesh wound. After a little time, I groped my way along in the darkness, feeling the wall as I went, till I came to the steps leading up from the water. Then I hurried home as well as my weakness would permit. I got into bed, and sent for the surgeon, who dressed the wound, and assured me it was not dangerous. To all inquiries as to how I came by the hurt, I declined to give any explanation.

"The next day, when the surgeon came to see me, I was as calm as usual—for my nature was not very excitable—and as I had no fever, and the wound was healing, he began to tell me the news of the morning. How some fishermen, at break of day, found a hat upon the quay, which was identified by the name in it to belong to George Masters. It was crushed in, and there were several clots of fresh blood upon it. The wet ground, too, bore the marks of feet, as if a violent struggle had taken place up to the very edge of the quay wall; and a short, loaded stick, of a very remarkable appearance, was found close to the scene of the struggle.

"But the strangest part of the story is," said the doctor, looking significantly at me, "that Masters cannot be found, and they say that the owner of the bludgeon is well known."

"When the doctor was gone, I rose and went to Grace Towers. I saw her alone, and told her all. What more passed between us I need not relate, but I left her with the determination never to disclose the circumstances of that night, whatever might be the consequences of my silence. On my way home I was apprehended by a constable, on a warrant, and brought before the justices who were then investigating the mysterious occurrence. It was proved that Masters had been seen going down the street towards the quay, and that I was afterwards observed going in the same direction, with a short stick in my hand. The hat was identified as Masters', and the stick as mine. I was asked if I wished to give any explanation, or to account for the facts which looked so suspicious, coupled with the disappearance of Masters, and my wound: but, cautioned of the consequences of doing so, I declined to give any explanation.

"This course created, as I knew it would, a very unfavourable impression against me, and I was detained in custody till I gave bail, to answer any charge that might be brought against me.

"Well, Grace and I were married: her aunt died a short time after, and we were left alone in our home. Lonely enough it was, and cheerless soon it became to me. From that fatal night a blight was upon my life. I, an innocent man, lay under the suspicion of a crime which a word could have dispelled. My former acquaintances shunned me. I was never of a temper to solicit friendships, and I resented treatment that was, after all, but natural. And so I became moody and sullen, all the more so that I saw my wife become daily more dejected, till I felt that an estrangement was growing between our lives. In a year a little one was born to us; but the mother never rose from the bed of sickness, and in a month I was left a solitary man. But solitude drove me to despair. I neglected my farm; I became reckless; and I sought, in the excitement of the bottle and the oblivion of drunkenness, a temporary relief from my disgust of life. One night, after market, I had been drinking to excess, at the 'Sun,' with such companions as my hospitality still procured me. One of them helped me home, and, aiding me to open the door with my latch-key, I staggered into the sitting-room, where he left me. I have a confused recollection of striking a light, which fell from my hand as I endeavoured to light a candle, and then stumbling up-stairs to bed, where I flung myself in my clothes, and fell into a deep, stupid sleep. How long I continued in that state I don't know, but I was awakened by a sense of suffocation. It was still dark, but the room was filled with thick smoke. I got out of bed, and, opening the door, found the place in flames all around me. How I got out I can't tell, but I found myself at last in the open air. My first thought was to rush to the town for assistance, for no farm servants lived with me. I hurried away, and had gone some distance, when I remembered that my child and her nurse were in a room in the back of the house. I returned, wild with terror, and had just entered the avenue, and got sight of the blazing house, then a sheet of flame. I heard the scream of a woman from the midst of the conflagration, and before I could reach the spot, the whole house had fallen with a dull crash—a shapeless mass of smoking and burning ruin. For a moment my senses failed me; then I came to myself, and rushed round the pile: but though the flames gave me light as of day, no human being was to be seen. Child and nurse were buried in the ruins!"

Mark Austin paused, overcome with emotion, and burying his head upon his arms on the table, sobbed aloud. After a time he recovered his composure, and resumed—

"Life was nothing now to me, and yet the instinct of life made me shrink from death. But to live any longer on the scene of all my miseries was horrible to think of. I fled away, as one who flies from the face of an enemy. For days and days I wandered on, I cared not where, so as it led me farther from the hated spot. The money that I chanced to have about me that night was more than usual, for I had sold some produce in the market. At last I found myself some hundred miles away. Then, with a portion of the money that remained, I purchased some pedlar's wares to trade on; and so I have for many, many weary years travelled, with a restless, Cain-like spirit, till I have wandered over the length and breadth of the land, but never coming near the one dreaded place, nor ever naming it—wishing to banish the recollection of it for ever from my mind.

"And now, George Masters, you that would have murdered my body, that have well-nigh murdered my soul, that made my wedded life wretched, that sent my wife pining to the grave, and have the death of my child on your head—you dare to ask me to forgive? Never! In the name of justice and of truth, I swear——"

"Sinner, madman, forbear!" cried the parson, as he sprang forward and placed his hand on the mouth of the speaker. "Vengeance belongs to God alone. Forbear, I say! John Godwin commands you!"

The two men gazed at their host with a mingled expression of terror and incredulity. Then he continued—

"Mark Austin and George Masters, look well at me. Time and sorrow may have changed me somewhat, but still you will not fail soon to recollect me. Ay, I see it is so. Now, hearken to what I have to tell, and when I have finished, then, Mark Austin, proceed with your unholy oath, if you dare! George Masters, you spoke the truth to-night, but not the whole truth. You promised to be to my mother as a son; but you promised more—to be to Grace as a brother, but only a brother, for you knew how dearly I loved her; and you swore you would guard her for me from all the world. Were you a true man when you suffered your own heart to love her; when, on a vague rumour of my death, in one short year you sought her love, instead of keeping my memory fresh in her heart, and encouraging her to hope even against hope? False to your oath, false to your friend! Have I not much to forgive? Mark Austin, you robbed me of her who was, in the sight of God, my wife; nay, more, you made her life sad by your coldness; and you reproached her for loving another, though you knew not who that other was. But you knew she married you to make comfortable the last days of a declining woman who was more than a mother to her; and you had no right to expect from her more than the duty she gave you. You brought her to her grave before her time, and you gave yourself up to intemperance, that cast you at last a homeless and a childless man upon the world. Now hear how mercifully God has dealt with you, even as he dealt with you in sparing your life. A long sickness fell upon me after I got to America, and brought me nigh unto death: then my letters were intercepted during the war. At length, after a prosperous venture, I returned home to make Grace my wife. I reached the town where I had left all that was dear to me on earth, to learn that my mother was dead, and that she I loved had become the wife of another, and was dead too. I should have sunk beneath the blow, but the hand of God upheld me. Then I determined to quit the spot for ever. But a strange desire impelled me, ere I went, to visit the grave where my love lay sleeping. And so, at the dead of night I went forth towards the churchyard beyond the town. As I passed the gate of the old manor-house, I was attracted by a blaze of light that suddenly shot up into the sky. I saw the house was in flames: I hurried up to it in time to hear the screams of a woman. Not a moment was to be lost; I burst open a window, rushed up a staircase, and, half-suffocated with smoke, I met a woman descending with a child in her arms. As I hurried them out by the way I had entered, the stairs sank in with a crash behind us. We fled for shelter to an outhouse at a little distance, and then a flood of lurid flame burst up into the air, and the house fell down in ruins. After a little time I brought my charge to the inn where I had stopped, and learned from the woman that I had saved the child of Grace.

All believed that the master of the house had perished in the flames; for his companion had told how he had helped him home drunk. Then I felt the great love and mercy of God in giving me the child of her I loved, and I vowed to him to dedicate my life to her happiness. I need not tell you how I devoted myself to the service of God, and entered into the ministry; how I settled in this quiet, lonely spot, with good old Sybil and Ruth, and seek my own happiness in making others happy. And now, Mark Austin, have I not much to forgive you too? Yes; and from my heart I forgive you both. Mark Austin, in the name of Him whose birth we shall soon be called to celebrate—who forgave his murderers, and with his dying lips prayed God to forgive them—I call upon you to forgive."

"'Tis hard, 'tis hard; and all at once, John Godwin!"

"Ay, all at once, and heartily, too. Mark Austin, would you, too, be a murderer?"

"Never!" said Austin, with horror. "I will never harm a hair of his head."

"Whosoever hateth his · brother is a murderer. Sinner! if you would be forgiven, forgive. As the servant of Him who declared, 'if ye forgive not men their tresspases, neither will your Father forgive your trespasses,' I command you to forgive."

"I forgive."

"Heartily, honestly, unreservedly?"

"Ay, with my whole heart. George Masters, your hand."

At this moment a sweet sound broke upon the stillness of night. John Godwin opened the shutters of the window, and threw up the sash, and then the chiming music of the merry Christmas bells came floating into the room, like the songs of holy angels that came to hallow the scene of reconciliation with their presence. The storm without had subsided, as it had in the hearts of those within, and the moon shone serenely down from a cloudless sky upon the pure white snow. Open burst the door, and a girl sprang in with a merry laugh—

"A happy Christmas to you, dear uncle! Do you hear the bells pealing the Christmas hymn?"

The sight of the strangers arrested the voice of the girl.

"'Tis Grace—'tis herself!" exclaimed the men.

"Not Grace, but Ruth Austin. Child, behold your long-lost father! Mark Austin, receive your child!"

Mark Austin sprang forward to clasp the child that fell trembling into his arms. After a moment John Godwin released her from his embrace, and laid her gently on the couch.

"Down on your knees, forgiven sinners! Down in the dust before the God of mercy and of love, this holy Christmas morning."

Then, raising his hands, he solemnly ejaculated—

"Glory to God in the highest,
And on earth peace, good-will towards men."

Innocents Day.

TURNED TO THE WALL.

CHAPTER I.

THE SMITHY.

CLING, clang! cling, clang! 'Tis a winter's night, in the month of January, well-nigh half a century ago, in a central county of merry England. Out upon the still, sharp, frosty air rings the beat of the smith's hammer, chiming pleasant music that shapes itself into song, as it did in the days of our first George to the ear of Handel, when he fixed the sounds into a melody and made them immortal. Out, too, upon the blackness of the dark, cold sky, flashes the ruddy glow of sparkling light through the open window of the smithy, flooding into the night in a sharply-defined stream,

with its banks of gloom bounding it at either side—
one of those pictures which old masters loved to
paint for the contrasts of light and shade. How
gratefully comes the sense of warmth and comfort
from within to him who stands outside in the chilly
air! some belated villager making his way homewards; some wanderer that knows not where to rest,
and hails the friendly blaze where he may find heat
and shelter. One such stands there now, and gazes
upon the bright interior. There is but one person
within—a tall, large-boned, athletic man: his coat
is off, and his shirt-sleeves, tucked up to the shoulders, display the toil-developed muscles of his hairy
arms. The roar from the nozzle of his bellows has
just subsided, and the smith, hammer in one hand,
and tongs in the other, plucks from the fire a bar
of red-hot iron, lays it on the anvil, and down
comes the heavy hammer, making the sparks fly all
around him. *Cling, clang! cling, clang!* and the
merry sounds ring out like a hymn of labour. And
a nobler subject for a hymn to God never warmed
an English heart! There are the two genii of the
lamp of England's glory—grim, and swart, and hard,
yet submissive and pliant to the hand of toil—IRON
and COAL. Men of England, let us bless God who
gave us—not the olive and the vine of Southern

Europe, nor the diamonds of Golconda, nor the pearls of Arabia, nor the gold-fields of Australia; but the ironstone and the coalfield—precious gifts, by which the brain of Science and the hand of Art have wrought out a nation's wealth and power.

The man paused at last, thrust the bar into the trough, where it hissed and sent up a white steam, and wiped his brow with the back of his hand. At this moment the spectator outside opened the door of the smithy. Before he could enter, the smith's voice assailed him—"Hollo! Dickon, where hast been this hour back? Plague on thee for an idle varlet; I'll be sworn thee'st been at every ale-house between this and the market-cross. I'm half-minded to give thee a taste of something stronger than——"

The smith stopped short in his threat as the light fell on the face of the stranger.

"Faith, I thought you were my 'prentice, Dickon Grimes. I sent the fellow, an hour since, for steel, into the village hard by, and I suppose he's been drinking. But you aint Dickon, I see."

"No, I'm not."

"So much the better for you. Who are you? What do you want?"

"I want a guide to the village."

"Well, I can't leave my work just now; but if

you wait till I finish this job for the squire, I'll put you on your road. I shouldn't be long if I had any one to help me. Can you handle a sledge?"

"I don't know—I'll try."

The stranger took off his coat, turned up his shirt-sleeves, and prepared for work. He was a young man in the early prime of life, well-built and light; but the white, though nervous, arm did not tell of much hard labour. The smith blew up the fire, and in a few moments another heated bar was on the anvil: and so the two went heartily to work.

"You'll do well enough," said the smith, as they stopped, flinging the bar into the trough. "Where do you come from?"

"From a long way off."

"You'll be a Cornishman by your voice."

"No, I'm from the North-country."

"Yorkshire, belike?"

"No, up near the borders."

"Where are you going?"

"To the village, if you'll show me the way."

The smith was no fool, but he saw he had met his match. So he gave it up and replied—

"Well, when these two bars are put in the gate,

my work will be done. Come, lend me a hand once more, and then I'm at your service."

"Now, good fellow," said the smith, when they had finished, "put on your coat, and come with me into the house. The good wife will have something comfortable, I'll warrant you."

"With all my heart!" was the ready response.

The smith led the way across a little plat of grass, fenced in with paling, to the door of a snug cottage; and they entered. A smart little matron stood by the fire, cooking, and turned round to give her husband a smiling welcome.

"Doll, my lass, here's a new 'prentice. Dickon has turned gentleman, and gone off to get drunk. Sit down, sit down, my lad!"

Little Dorothy Meadowes looked up at the newcomer, and she saw with the tail of her eye that he wasn't just the stuff that blacksmiths are made of, and then she smiled and blushed like a little coquette, as she was, and bid him welcome.

And so they sat down to supper. The smith fell upon his trencher manfully—'twas a labour of love. The stranger ate more sparingly; and when the host, after a hearty pull at the tankard, pushed it to his guest, the latter turned to his hostess and said, "Fair

Mistress Dorothy, I drink to your health and our better acquaintance." Whereat Dorothy smiled and blushed again, and John Meadowes broke out into a roar, thinking, good soul, that he had hoaxed his wife about the new 'prentice; but he hadn't, though. After a little the man grew thoughtful, and, seeming to forget where he was, began to hum slowly a sweet wild air. The woman looked keenly at him, and then said to her husband, "John, you were late at work to-night; something more will do you no harm; but you must go and draw it for yourself, for you know I'm a little weakly just now."

The big smith looked at his little wife tenderly, and went out of the room. As he returned, he saw Dorothy withdrawing her hand from the stranger's, who was speaking to her in a low, earnest voice.

"Hollo!—I say! Hands off there, my fine fellow—that's work I want nobody to help me with. It seems to come easier to you than sledging iron."

"Nay, nay, John!" said little Dorothy. "What! jealous because a young man is civil to your wife!" and she ran over and took the two dark, horny hands of her husband in her own, and looked up with a long, clear, innocent gaze into his eyes, till the gloom fled out of them.

"Well, well, get thee away, lass! I suppose it's only his North-country manners."

"And now, friend, I'm ready for the road."

"But mind you don't go into the 'Blue Boar,' John. Promise me."

"Well, I promise thee, Doll—there's my pledge!" and the smith kissed the red lips of his little wife.

The two men went out into the dark night, and left little Dorothy Meadowes alone. When the door was closed, she sat down, put her head between her hands, and had a hearty fit of crying.

CHAPTER II.

THE "BLUE BOAR" OF BROKELEIGH.

IF you were let down from a balloon upon the green of Brokeleigh, you would know at a glance that you were in an English village. Warm brick houses, with their red-tiled roofs and trim gardens in front, surrounded three sides of the neat, grassy plot of some two acres, enclosed with wooden palings painted white. The fourth side was open to the river, near the bank of which rose a long, high mass of stone building perforated with innumerable windows. Unmistakably English was this busy hive of human labour—a cotton mill. But if you could have any doubt of your whereabouts, turn to your right, and walk along the village street till you come to the cross, and look about you. There is the market-house, a heavy, unsightly, square building, of dark stone. A colonnade of pillars support circular arches all around, giving entrance to the ground floor, where a market was held weekly, and sustaining the upper storey, which discharged, in turn, the duties of a town hall, a court of justice, and an assembly room. A low, square tower rose from the centre of the roof, surmounted by a vane in the similitude of a cock, of so conservative and unbending a disposition, that he scorned to be influenced by any atmospheric changes, and didn't care a bean what way the wind blew—the parish church, and the parish stocks, and the thoroughly English inn completed the picture.

The morning sun was shining redly through the frosty fog, as Dorothy Meadowes walked at the top of her speed across the common. On she pressed to the town, and up the High street, till she came to the market-cross, and stood opposite the "Blue Boar." From a pole that projected out of the wooden balcony of that ancient fabric, swung a square sign-board, whereon was depicted the animal that gave its name to the principal inn of Brokeleigh. That rampant and grisly beast had been standing—nobody knows for how many generations—on his hind legs, defiant alike of the laws of gravity and the endurance of muscle, with golden tusks, bright cobalt body, and bristling mane; and round his neck a golden collar with a chain that trailed away in all manner of impossible curves to the ground. In passed little Dorothy, heedless of the grim old porker over her head, stealthily, as if to avoid observation. This was not to be: a cheery voice from the bar saluted her,

"Good morning, Mrs. Meadowes; you aint going to pass an old friend without a word with him, sure? 'Tis an age since I saw you, and you look as blooming as ever."

Dorothy turned round to where burly Abel Dobbs sat, framed and glazed, within the bar window.

"Ah, Mr. Dobbs, good morning. I didn't expect to see you so early: and how is your missus?"

Abel made a wry face. "Oh, lively: scrubbing, and washing, and turning the house inside out. We shall have a plaguy stirring life of it, I'm thinking."

"Well, I'll just run in and see her."

"Aye, do, and be sure to tell John to look in to-morrow. I want a word with him. We'll fight as pretty a main of cocks as ever he saw in his life."

Dorothy tripped into the house, but she did not go down the passage that led to the kitchen. No; she hurried up-stairs, ran along the corridor, and knocked softly at the door of "the Angel." 'Twas quickly opened by the occupant of the room, and exposed to view the face of a man—the very man that had taken her hand the night before. In glided Dorothy, and the door was closed behind her. Ah, little Dorothy, what a sad little lass for gossiping you are! May the good Angel have you in his keeping!

Not many minutes after, the Angel began to pull his bell violently, and Mrs. Dobbs, who *chanced* to be in the next room putting things in order, declared afterwards, that she heard suppressed sobbing, as of a woman, and that when she ran to the door she found it bolted inside. The occupant of the room came to the door and asked for a glass of brandy-and-water, a hand was put out to receive it, and the door was shut again. In about half-an-hour afterwards Dorothy Meadowes slipt out quietly, and went down-stairs, and then she hurried past the bar and into the street. It was fortunate for her that Abel Dobbs had gone out to have a talk with a neighbour, else he would surely have seen that little Dorothy's face was flushed with agitation, and her eyes red with weeping. Dorothy did not turn homewards, but she went through one of the arches of the market-house, and under the conservative cock, and right through, out at the other side, up the road that led to the Vicarage, and slipt in through the back-door of the house. What brought her to the Vicarage? Was it to gossip with old Mrs. White, the housekeeper? May be so: for Mrs. White was a great gossip, and loved dearly a long talk about everybody's business. If that was Dolly's occupation, they must have discussed the affairs of the whole country side; for a good hour had passed before she shook hands with the old lady at the door, and at last turned her steps homewards. Then Dolly slipt quietly into the pretty cottage, where we found her at first, divested herself of her cloak and bonnet, and was soon busily occupied preparing the noon-day meal for her husband. Ah! true-hearted John Meadowes! you and your rakish 'prentice, Dickon Grimes, have been blowing and sledging away since breakfast, not dreaming that little Dolly has been all the morning gadding and gossiping through the village, and been closeted with —Heaven knows whom.

CHAPTER III.

THE HALL.

'Tis midday—the 28th of December, "The Innocents Day"—clear, bright, and frosty—for the mist has rolled away, and the sun is shining from a cloudless sky—as a man walks through the green of Brokeleigh, and down to the river-side. He crosses the steep old bridge: he does not take the highway to the right or left, but goes straight forward to the great antique entrance to Brokeleigh Hall. A heavy iron gate stands between two massive square piers of rusticated masonry, vermiculated and weather-stained, each surmounted by a boar, the cognizance of the De Brokeleighs.

A ring at the wicket summons the gate-keeper's wife, who, with a curtsey, admits the visitor. A cheery greeting, a kind word of inquiry for the good man and the children, and he passes on up the broad, straight avenue of noble chestnut-trees. A few words will make you acquainted with the man, so that you shall know the Vicar of Brokeleigh before he reaches the Hall.

You see a tall, thin, sinewy man, under thirty years of years age, with a face pale and emaciated, a forehead high and white—all the whiter for the masses of raven hair that fall on either side—and the black, piercing eyes that glitter from beneath his bushy eyebrows. His face, when in repose, has an air of sternness, almost of asceticism; but when he speaks, a rich musical voice, and, at times, a smile of peculiar sweetness playing about his lips, tell of a noble and benevolent nature. Newton Herbert took a double first at Oxford, and was a fellow of his college: the family borough was at his command, and his friends looked upon him as one who would yet take a prominent place among the statesmen of his day. But he suddenly changed his mind, took holy orders, and, declining a metropolitan chaplaincy, accepted the offer of his father's old friend, and buried himself amongst the primitive folks of the remote parish of Brokeleigh. Two years of earnest, manful labour had wrought wonders in the parish. Vice and immorality he assailed with unsparing vigour. In the pulpit he denounced the sin with a power so pointed, that the sinner, though unnamed, was conscious he was meant, and trembled at the thought of the visit, which he well knew the vicar would pay him next day, and the reproof, sharp and severe, which he would administer. With the penitent he was gentle and consoling, and at the bedside of the reformed profligate he soothed the departing soul, that he had at first awakened to a sense of guilt by his stern denunciations, and then softened by the offers of mercy and pardon. And so Newton Herbert was feared, loved, and honoured by all.

And now he has passed up the stone steps that lead to the terrace, from which the old Hall rises with arched doorway and mullioned window, and turret and gable, and steep roof; and in another moment he is seated in the library, awaiting the appearance of the master of the house.

A man of about fifty years of age enters. He is above the middle height, strong built, and inclining to stoutness, with a face somewhat florid, that tells of exposure to wind and weather. His bearing is frank and manly; but you soon detect an air of something that looks like pride, and an expression of firmness amounting almost to obstinacy, with now and then a shade of sadness passing over his features. This is Roger de Brokeleigh, of Brokeleigh Hall, with Norman blood in his veins, whose fountain-head is to be sought for in the fields of Crescy and Agincourt—Brokeleigh of Brokeleigh, as he is called by his acquaintances, and better known as "the squire" in the neighbourhood for miles round. A fine specimen in his way of the old English country gentleman (whose characteristic peculiarities were even then dying out before the equalising influence of increasing knowledge); full of class prejudices, proud of his lineage, and somewhat exacting of the respect due to it; standing stoutly by his order; hospitable, generous, loving, and kind to his tenantry, whose rights he will suffer no one to invade; but whose votes at vestry or hustings he considers his own property, resisting the progress of democratic power and the innovations of popular institutions; believing in handlooms and spinning wheels, and hating mills and machinery.

Herbert is gazing thoughtfully upon the fire in the antique grate as the squire enters, and, coming up to him, cordially extends his hand.

"Delighted to see you, my dear Herbert. Anything new in these days of novelties? Have the slaters repaired the roof of the Vicarage for you, as I directed?"

"Not yet, Sir. They are all employed at present at Mr. Plant's new school-house. I can wait very well, as long as this fine weather lasts."

"Wait! Why should my work wait on Mr. Plant's? Besides, I do not see what need there is for a new school-house at Brokeleigh? Is not mine well managed? I never heard of any complaint."

"Excellently managed: but the population has lately increased a good deal."

"Ay, and whose fault is that? Doesn't it all come of that fellow, Plant, and his new-fangled mill, bringing vagrants from the country round to work at it?"

"Not vagrants, Mr. De Brokeleigh, but hard-working men and women with their families. Mr. Plant is an honest, intelligent, energetic man, that does much good. He gives the people a great deal of employment, and fair wages."

"Ay, and works them from morning to night in close, unwholesome rooms. Look at the little factory children's faces and hands, white and thin from toil and confinement—poor things! They ought to be red and chubby at out-door work in the fields."

"I have spoken to Mr. Plant on these matters, and suggested an improved mode of ventilating the rooms, and asked him to shorten the time of the children's labour, and I must say he readily and cheerfully adopted my views. 'Twas his own proposal to build the school-house. He said to me, in his own blunt, business-like way, 'If I get so much out of the little ones' bodies, it is only fair that I should put something into their minds, and so make the debit and credit sides of my books balance.' 'Twas a sentiment worthy of an honest English employer."

"Well, well, we'll see. I suppose it is for the good of the people's health he has built this big chimney that is to fill the air with soot and smoke?"

"'Tis for his own good, Sir. The river, though flooded in winter, is too low in summer to work his new machinery."

"May be so, but I shall see whether his good or the good of Brokeleigh is to be preferred. I shall try and present it as a nuisance."

"Take my advice, Sir, and do no such thing. Depend upon it, we cannot—and we ought not if we could—resist the spirit of enterprise and improvement that is making our people prosperous and great."

"Pardon me, Mr. Herbert, I must decline to take your advice in matters where my own rights are concerned. I shall certainly try to resist this that you are pleased to call an improvement. Why, Sir, I shan't be safe from the annoyance, even up here. Come into my room, and look at it, and judge for yourself."

The squire opened a door at the far end of the library, and crossing a retired corridor, led the vicar into an apartment at the other side of the house.

CHAPTER IV.

THE SQUIRE'S ROOM.

THE room into which the vicar and his host entered was known from time immemorial as "The Squire's Room." It was an apartment of moderate size, panelled in oak to the ceiling, and decidedly what may be called snug. In this the lords of the manor of Brokeleigh had for generations ensconced themselves as their private sanctum. Except the servants to arrange the room, and the steward occasionally to settle his accounts, or receive his master's directions, few persons had access into this apartment; indeed, Herbert now entered it for the first time. He and the squire went to the window, where they had a full view of the obnoxious chimney, and discussed its merits and demerits, both in a utilitarian and sanitary point of view. Between men who, on many questions of the day, entertained sentiments widely differing, and each likely to take decided views, it was not very probable that the discussion would make a convert of either to the opinions of the other. At length, Herbert turned away with a sigh, and glanced at some of the pictures on the wall.

A portrait of a young man in regimentals attracted his attention, and he stepped over to examine it.

"Ah, you are looking at Reginald's picture," said the squire. "I had a letter from him lately from India; he is daily in expectation of his majority."

"I am glad to hear it, Sir. The prosperity of a child is always a happiness to a father's heart. Children are a great blessing."

"No doubt, and sometimes a great care," replied the squire, with a sigh. "There is Charley's portrait beyond. To-day, you know, he is of age, and he is coming home to celebrate his birthday. I expect him in the afternoon; we shall have a little fête to greet him."

"So I understand. And what's this, Sir?"

As he asked the question, Herbert stood opposite a picture-frame that was placed between the two others, but the face of the picture was turned to the wall.

"Ha! a woman!" he exclaimed, as he reversed the frame: "and a lovely one too."

The squire sprang forward, and thrust Herbert violently some paces back.

"Sir—Sir, this presumption is intolerable! By what right do you dare to interfere with the arrangements of my house—to pry into my secrets?"

Herbert drew himself up to his full height, his pale face flushed for a moment under the sense as of an indignity; but it was only for a moment, the flush passed away, and left him pale and calm as before. Then he gazed upon De Brokeleigh sadly, almost sternly, as he replied, with quiet solemnity, "By the right, Sir, which I derive from Him whose commission I bear—of Him from whom no secrets are hid. By that right do I seek to look into the secret which like an ulcer is eating into your life, that I may, with His blessing, cleanse and heal it." And then the sweet smile played about his mouth as he added, in the tenderest accents of gentleness and affectionate respect, "By the right, too, of one who loves you as a son loves a father—who loves you so faithfully that he braves your anger to do you a service, as he would lay down his life to save yours. Oldest and best friend of my dear father, open your heart to me, as you would to him, I entreat you."

The squire sank down on a seat, and buried his face in his hands. There was a silence of many minutes. A conflict of passions was raging within him more fierce than if it had exploded in audible demonstrations. 'Tis over, and the better nature of the man prevails.

"Herbert, you have for two years past been a loving son to me, while the sons that I love were forced to be absent, and left me childless. Yes, I will tell you the secret which I had meant to take down with me to the grave. Sit down and hear me."

CHAPTER V.

THE SQUIRE'S TALE.

"You say truly, Herbert; she was a lovely woman—lovelier than even she looks in that picture. When my wife died, many years ago, she left me three children, two sons, as you know, and a daughter—the girl whose portrait you have just been looking at. The love I bore my dear Alice would have gone down into the grave with her, but that her little pet, Lucy, was left—so like, and yet so unlike, her mother—to sport about me, and keep the love of woman from dying out altogether from my heart. To the love for the pretty child was, as she grew up, added the pride in the lovely woman. I indulged her every wish; I procured her every accomplishment; I lavished on her whatever wealth could procure. To tell you that she was admired throughout the country, would be needless. I knew well that, with the advantages of birth and fortune which she possessed, I had but to choose amongst the best blood of the land for her husband. Well, from time to time she went up to London to a relative, a widow lady, both to avail herself of the best masters, and to enjoy the society of the metropolis. My tastes were all centred in the country and in my own people, and so I seldom accompanied her. Upon her last return home—it is now more than three years ago—I told her one evening of an eligible suitor for her hand, and expressed my desire that she should receive his addresses. Judge of my astonishment, when she declared to me it was impossible! I asked, with some impatience, how she could so speak. Had I not chosen a man in every way worthy of her? She admitted he was unobjectionable; but— 'But what?' I asked, with displeasure. Her only reply, for a time, was tears. I grew angry; I charged her with disobedience; I reminded her of her duty to her parent; that I expected implicit obedience; and that I *should* be obeyed. Then the girl dashed away her tears, and, drawing herself up proudly—it was the first time I had ever seen her show an unruly spirit—answered; 'I will obey you in all things in which you have a right to require obedience; but in this, I am not bound to obey. I cannot obey: I love another!' Indignation and amazement kept me, for a moment, tongue-tied. 'Love another!' I exclaimed. 'Child, you dare not; and without my knowledge!' 'Alas!' said she, 'almost without my own.' Then I learned the humiliating story:—A young man—a painter, from whom she took lessons—some penniless fellow, who, for aught I knew, or cared to know, had not a drop of good blood in his veins, dared to win her affections, and disclosed his love at their last interview, and—and—I blush to own it—received the assurance of her's in return."

De Brokeleigh hung down his head, and was silent: the avowal of the indignity oppressed him with shame. Herbert turned away his face; he would not witness the proud man's emotion; but he dared not express a sympathy with a feeling of which he disapproved; and so did not speak.

"Why should I dwell upon the painful scene that passed. To my commands, my anger, my threats, she opposed a strong and obstinate resistance; till at last I vowed, in my displeasure, that I would force obedience by my authority, as I had failed to win it by my love; and so we parted for the night. Next day Lucy did not make her appearance. Her maid, who was her foster-sister, brought a message from her mistress, begging to be excused from coming down on the plea of indisposition. And so I was left to myself to meditate alone; for my sons were both away at the time, Reginald with his regiment, and Charles in College. A sleepless night did not serve to calm my irritation. I felt that my best feelings had been outraged; that my love had met with ingratitude; that my parental authority had been set at nought: and so the more I thought over the scene of the evening before, the more indignant I felt, and the more determined to carry my point. The day passed over without our meeting; but late in the evening Lucy entered the room where I was sitting, looking pale and wretched; and flinging herself at my feet, besought me to hear her. My heart yearned to take her to it—for 'tis a hard thing, Herbert, to drive the love for a child out of a father's heart—but I crushed down my emotion as a guilty weakness, and answered coldly, I would hear nothing but her submission. Then she rose slowly, and said:

"'Father, I cannot: anything but this.'

"'This,' I replied, 'or nothing. In three days my friend comes here as your suitor. When you are prepared to obey me, I shall see you again; till then we part;' and, waving her from me, I rose and left the room. Two days after this, and still Lucy gave no sign of submitting to my will. I learned from her maid that she was feverish, and had spent so restless a night, that the girl had called in the family doctor to see her. The day wore on as the rest; and I occupied myself a good deal out of doors. I sat up unusually late that night, looking over some family papers, and had just risen to retire, when I was startled by the report of fire-arms at the far side of the house. I threw up one of the windows in the room, stepped out on the terrace, and hurried round to the place from which the sound came. There I saw a dark object lying on the ground, and a man, at a little distance, with a gun in his hand, standing over it. I called out to him, and he answered, and then I recognised one of my game-keepers; the dark object was a man, weltering in his blood! We raised him; he was quite dead. I saw how it was at once. The keeper had, as I directed him, been on the watch for some time past, to catch the poachers that were destroying my preserves. Passing near the house, as he told me, he saw a figure moving stealthily along; he challenged him, when the man began to run away. The keeper called upon him to stop and surrender, but in vain; and he then ran forward, and overtook him: a struggle ensued, and the keeper fired. By this time some of the servants, who had also heard the shot, joined us, and I had the corpse brought into an out-house, which

I locked, till the morning, when an inquest was holden. The gamekeeper deposed to the facts I have mentioned, and the jury found that the keeper had acted in the discharge of his duty, and in self-defence. No one identified the body, and I gave orders for its interment. As I sat down to breakfast, Lucy's maid rushed wildly in, crying. As soon as she was able to speak, she told me that when she went to Lucy's room, a few minutes since, she found the bed had not been occupied, and her mistress nowhere to be found. I desired the girl to be silent, and then repaired to the room. As I drew back the curtain of the bed, a sealed note upon the pillow caught my eye; I thrust it into my pocket, went to my bedchamber, and, tearing it open, the mystery was disclosed. The wretched girl had fled with her lover; and that lover—the horrible conviction flashed in a moment across my mind—was the corpse that lay outside. I sank down upon a chair as if stricken by a thunderbolt, and it was many minutes before I could recover myself so as to think calmly on what was to be done. The first thing was to make search for my child. I hurried out to give orders for that purpose, when one of the farm-labourers met me with a shawl in his hand. It was dripping wet; and he stated he had drawn it out of the river, about a mile below the bridge, where he saw it floating. I recognised it instantly as Lucy's; and, though ready to sink, I mastered myself, by a strong effort, that I might not betray my emotion before the man. Herbert, Herbert, I cannot proceed with the details! All search was fruitless: and I felt that the girl, who, no doubt, had left the house with her lover, had fled away when he was shot, and had either thrown herself in despair or fallen accidentally into the river, then swollen with the winter's flood, and was swept away to the sea. The story that went abroad, to which the account of the doctor and the maid gave some plausibility, was, that Miss De Brokeleigh had been in fever, and, in a moment of delirium had escaped from her room, and wandered to the river, where she was drowned. From that day her name has not passed my lips till now, and no one ventures to speak it in my presence. On that day I turned her portrait to the wall, to shut her out from my sight if I may not from my thoughts."

It was a long time before the silence that followed this sad revelation was broken. At length Herbert rose, and approaching his host, took his hand respectfully, and said:

"Sir, I feel for you profoundly. If you have erred, God has heavily punished that error. Even from this take comfort. May I speak freely, both as God's minister and as your true friend?"

The squire drew his hand away quickly, as if pained by Herbert's words. Then, recovering his composure, he said, with something of his wonted spirit,

"Speak, Mr. Herbert. I am sure that in neither character will you forget what is due to yourself or to me."

"When I said, Sir, that you erred, I felt how sorely you were tried. God, who has punished your sin, will doubtless remember how much you loved. The past is irrevocable: we look to it but to warn us for the future; and so I bid you to take comfort. When you and the daughter you loved and lost shall meet hereafter—as in the greatness of God's mercy I confidently believe you shall—she will know and confess that she was not blameless, while you will admit that you taxed her obedience beyond a father's right."

"It may be that I did. But did she not destroy all my cherished hopes? Did she not count my love as nothing, compared with a light fancy of an hour?"

"Yes; and deeply she has suffered for it! But remember that the same divine teaching that says, 'Children, obey your parents in all things,' adds, 'Fathers, provoke not your children, lest they be discouraged.'"

There was a long pause. "Dear and honoured friend," resumed the vicar, "I know you feel the truth of what I have said in the discharge of my duty. Let me solemnly put this test to your heart and conscience. If it were possible that the grave could yield up that lost child, and give her to you now, would you not take her to your arms as lovingly as ever?"

"I would! I would!" sobbed the man, in a burst of unwonted feeling, "all forgiven, all forgotten—all!"

"My father! my father!" and one rushed forward, and flung herself on his bosom, sobbing and wailing; and then she slid down to the ground on her knees, and clasped his limbs in her arms, and wept exceeding bitterly.

Herbert turned away, and left them. Let us do so likewise. The joy and the sorrow of that meeting are too sacred for other eyes than their own.

CHAPTER VI.

WE are again in the library. The father knows not, and cares not yet to ask, how all this has come to pass. He only knows and feels that his daughter lives, and sits beside him. After a time, Herbert entered, and he says to Lucy,

"It is time you should go."

"Go?" asked the father, in amazement. "Why, where? Is she not at home once more? Who shall take her from me again?"

"Father," said Lucy, rising, "my home is with my husband; for him alone would I leave you."

"Husband! husband! Who is he? Where is he?"

"He is here," said Herbert, as he opened the door. A young man, in the prime of life, walked forward, and stood beside Lucy, who put her hand in his. The squire drew himself up haughtily.

"Sir, may I ask by what right you enter my house, or approach my daughter? Who are you, Sir?"

"Mr. De Brokeleigh, I am that daughter's husband; by that right I take her hand. I confess I have no right to enter your house."

"May I request, then, Sir, that you will leave it."

The young man looked with tender sadness at Lucy, and then replied, respectfully,

"Sir, you shall be obeyed. I ask your pardon for my intrusion. Come, Lucy." De Brokeleigh moved forward to separate them.

"Nay," said Herbert; "this may not be, Sir. Whom God has joined together, let no man put asunder. In God's name, I require you to learn what the husband of your daughter has to say."

"Father, in the name of my dead mother—the wife whom you loved—hear my husband, for his wife's sake!"

"Proceed, Sir," said the squire, as he motioned the young man to a chair, and sat down himself; "I am ready to hear you."

"Mr. De Brokeleigh, you will ask how a poor painter dared to love your daughter? I dared to do so, in obedience to the instinct that God implanted in my nature, when he taught my eye and my heart to delight in all that was lovely and good in His creation. How I dared to tell that love, I scarcely know. I had determined to keep the secret within my heart forever; but when she gave me her hand, at what I believed was to be our last meeting on earth, love and despair overmastered me, and I spoke, in the deepest respect and humility, that love which, after all, could never dishonour her. The avowal that she returned my love filled me with joy, and I resolved that, if circumstances ever permitted, as I hoped they would, I would seek her at your hands. That resolution you forced me to abandon, when Lucy informed me that you not only forbade your daughter to marry a man she loved, but commanded her to receive the addresses of another. I lost not an hour in coming hither with a faithful servant. I contrived to see Lucy for a few moments, and arranged her flight with me in the night. We succeeded; but the poor fellow who remained behind to watch, lest the alarm might be given, and to mislead you should you seek to follow us, was shot by your gamekeeper. This very soon led, as also the finding of Lucy's shawl, which fell as she crossed the bridge, to the report of her death. Pardon me, Sir, for saying we had reason to think that, for a time at least, it would be better not to undeceive you. Within a few hours, I placed your daughter in the care of an aged female relative, where she remained till I made her my wife. Then we went to Germany, where I contrived to earn a livelihood, partly as an artist, and partly as a teacher of English: with no sorrow to come between our love, no cloud to dim its sunshine but the one unceasing yearning of my wife for her father's love, the one craving desire for his forgiveness. At last, circumstances lately occurred which enabled us to return to England, and we determined, at all risks, to seek pardon and reconciliation. Last evening we reached the village, and learning that Lucy's foster-sister was married to your smith, I contrived, by a stratagem, to get into her house, and make myself known to her. To-day, by her advice, we had a conference with Mr. Herbert, and told him all. With the assistance of Dorothy Meadowes, we gained an entrance into your house. Oh! Sir, it is for you to say are we to leave it for ever? The husband of the child you have received again from the dead entreats that you will pardon him too!"

"An unknown man, without birth, or means, or position," muttered the squire, as if reasoning with himself, "to receive *him* as the husband of a De Brokeleigh! 'tis too hard. I cannot! I cannot!"

"Yes, Sir, you can—hard as it is, you can—as a man of sense, you can: as a Christian, you must! If this young man springs from the people, he has their virtues—manliness, energy, self-reliance. He has won your child, and supported her by his industry: he has genius and education and honour and truth. Look back, Sir, a few generations, and you will find that half our peers were made of such stuff. If he wants wealth, you can supply it. This man, Sir, is worthy to be your daughter's husband, and to be your son."

Roger De Brokeleigh threw himself back in his chair, and covered his face with his hands. A terrible conflict was being waged in the head and heart of the man. Pride, obstinacy, prejudice, anger, shame, occupied every stronghold. Truth, reason, justice, mercy, and love—all-potent, thrice-blessed love!—assailed them. And angels—and greater than angels, it may be—looked down upon that spiritual battle-field. The fight is long and wavering; but at last the light has conquered the darkness, and the man rises to his feet, liberated from the thraldom of his baser nature.

"Sir," said he, extending his hand, "let the past be

forgotten. My daughter's husband is welcome to my house."

The young man took the squire's hand, and raised it respectfully to his lips.

Then said Herbert, solemnly, repeating a portion of the lesson for that morning's Service, "'And there is hope in thine end, saith the Lord, that thy children shall come again to their own border.' Sir Walter Marley, I give you joy!"

"Marley! Marley!" exclaimed the squire, in astonishment. "What, are you son of Sir Jasper Marley, of the North? I knew him when a boy."

"No, Sir; he was my uncle. His younger brother, my father, displeased him by marrying a penniless woman, who had no recommendations but beauty and worth. They never met afterwards, and, when I was left an orphan, at eighteen years of age, I scorned to seek his aid. Not many months since, his only son was killed by a fall from his horse, and a few posts afterwards brought me the intelligence of my uncle's death, by which I became entitled to the estates and baronetcy. I hastened from Germany. My rights were at once recognised, and I was no sooner put in possession of my property than we hastened hither. As your daughter loved me for myself, so I determined to owe nothing to my position in seeking your favour."

A sound of wheels crunching the gravel, and the loud cheers of many voices, interrupted the discourse, and the next moment a young man was in the arms of his father. I don't mean to tell all that followed—why should I?—the joyful surprise at finding a dead sister restored; the frank embrace of the new brothers; nor how Dorothy Meadowes slipt into the room, her eyes laughing with pleasure, and her husband, too, whom she beckoned from outside; how Sir Walter kissed her before John's face, and shook John stoutly by the hand, and asked when he should have another job for him. There were great doings that night in Brokeleigh: tar-barrels, bonfires, dancing, and what-not. Abel Dobbs' ale barrels flowed away till there was not a drop left in them, dancing on the green, and junketting in the great servants' hall. And Reuben Plant—like a fine, honest fellow, who bore no grudge, and honoured a true Englishman, whether he was peer or peasant—lit up his mill in a blaze of light with a huge lantern on the top of the obnoxious chimney. And the portrait of Lucy was never again TURNED TO THE WALL!

New Year's Eve.

SNOWED UP.

OF all the changes that seasons and elements work on the fair face of nature, I know none so complete and so sudden, as that wrought by a snow-fall at night. The last glimpse which we caught yesterday evening of the world without us, as the grey-headed butler closed the shutters and drew the curtains, exhibited to us the lawn of Castle Slingsby, still dressed in the robes of nature, worn-out and faded as they were. The long, coarse grass, rotted by the rains, and blanched by the wind, waved in the whistling blast of the evening, while, in another place, a rich sheltered nook continued still to make a very respectable show of green, struggling on through the assaults of winter, that it might be able to meet the next spring with an appearance of healthfulness and verdure—just as we see some old *beaux* about town, making themselves up, and taking all manner of care of themselves, that they may come out strong for the next campaign. More distant still, we caught a peep of the rich, brown mould of the ploughed field, through which the blade of the young corn had not yet come up, and beyond the next hedge lay the yet unbroken ridges, yellow since the preceding autumn; and, at the other side, were the sheep-pastures, with the grass cropt down short and bare, with here and there a spot round which the sheep were gathered, covered with the green food which the providence of the farmer had treasured up for the time when "the earth giveth not her increase." The dreariness of winter, too, was chequered by the unfading green of the various tribes of the fir-trees that still kept up a look of cheeriness and comfort— Mark Tapleys in their own way, coming out jolly under their trials. How warm and lusty they looked amid the sapless poles and bare branches of ash, and elm, and beech-tree. The holly, and the myrtles, too, how snug they looked in their lowly estate, never envying their lordly neighbours, when the blast went by and shook their proud heads, and stripped them of their glory. A leaf or two still lingered in seared brightness upon the oak and copper-beech; shrivelled and red, it twisted upon its stem, and with the next blast fell twirling to the ground amongst its dead companions. Beyond all, and closing in the landscape, as we took our last look at it, stood the far-away blue hills, standing out sharply against the frosty sky. But when the shutters were closed, and the curtains drawn, and we sat in the early night round the blazing hearth, we took little note of what the north-west wind and the dull, cloudy heavens, were working for us without. When we looked out the next morning, through the same windows, how changed was the scene of the day before! The dimmed sun struggled vainly to pierce the heavy clouds from which the thick snow fell like a white mist, contracting the view on every side. The varied hues of earth, the changeful face of nature, light and shadow, cloud and sunshine, all were hidden from the eye. It would seem as though during the night Nature had died, and morning's light beheld her arrayed, by unseen spirit, in her pallid death-shroud. Trackless snows lay on all around, concealing pasture, and fallow, and tillage, covering alike with its white mantle green shrubs and bare brances, as the undiscriminating graves does alike the aged dead and him who falls in the vigour of his manhood.

"Snowed up, by Jupiter!" cried old Jonathan Freke.

"There'll be nothing for it I guess, to-day, but cheroots and one's feet on the hobs. Saul, do you know how to make gin-sling or cocktail?—capital things in cold weather."

"No," said Saul; "but Mrs. Sampson is famous for cherry-bounce. Well, Abigail, there's an end to your projected pilgrimage to the fairy-well."

"And for my walk to Carrigbawn," said I.

"Just the day for the newspapers, or a page of Horace," said Professor Chubble, who, of course, affected classicality. "Vides, ut alta stet nive candidum."

"Or for a story," said I, remembering the Professor's talent that way.

"Yes, provided *you* tell it," retorted he, somewhat maliciously.

"A challenge, a challenge!" said Uncle Saul: "the Professor is entitled to call upon you."

"Well," said I, "I accept the challenge. Give me till noon."

"Agreed."

When noon came, the wind had shifted to the east, the sun broke through the sky, and scattering the humid clouds, shone down brightly on the world's vast and dreary expanse, all white, yet sublime and solemn in its monotony with the hills, standing close around, like white-robed giants. So we all went out for a walk, and, by common consent, I obtained a respite till evening. When the candles were lighted, and we drew round the fire, I told them this story.

BALANCING THE BOOKS.

CHAPTER I.

THE ERROR IN THE TOT.

"THERE'S something in those figures that I can't make out at all," said Goggles, giving his wig a poke that set it all awry.

"The devil's in them," said Kennedy, impatiently.

"I don't know as to that, Sir," replied the clerk, who never admitted anything in an account that was not capable of arithmetical demonstration, and not knowing the precise numerical value of Satan, on the debit side of a merchant's books (I don't think he even knew "the number of the beast"), he contented himself with saying, "I don't know that, Sir; but whatever it be, I'll find it out, with the blessing of God, before I go to bed to-night."

And so he drew down his spectacles once more upon his nose, and fell to work at the rebellious figures, muttering indistinctly to himself in the process of "totting;" while Kennedy, tilting backwards the high stool upon which he sat, till his shoulders rested against the wall behind him, began swinging his pendant legs to and fro. At first the movement was rapid and impatient, but by degrees it became slow and regular. One would say it had a tranquillising effect upon the man; for after a little he laid his right hand upon his chin, supporting the elbow with his left palm, and turning his eyes towards the ceiling, with a sigh, he gave himself up to some reverie or another.

While the merchant is musing, and the clerk is at his "tot," let us look at the picture before us. We shall have time enough to take in all the principal objects, and mark the lights and shades, before Goggles is half way down that long page of three columns—pounds, shillings, and pence.

You see a square room, not over lofty, and rather dingy. There is a bluish-grey paper, veined and marked into squares in the pattern, to imitate marble; its continuity is sadly marred by the insertion of a large iron safe in the wall, shelves, filled with account-books, a sheet almanack, and several *filasses* suspended from nails, upon which are invoices, bills of lading, and such other papers as form the decoration of a merchant's office. Against the wall, opposite the fire-place, stands an antique bureau, with drawers beneath and a slanting top, while an old-fashioned leather-bottomed chair flanks it at either side. There is a large, high, double-desk, one end of which is set close to the window; upon the top of it are two heavy brass candlesticks, the lights from which (for it is night) throw a partial illumination over the apartment, and bring out the two men, who are sitting one at each side of the desk, in strong relief. The face of the merchant is upturned, and so it catches all the light. We can read that face as we would read a book. The forehead is broad, and goes sheer up like a wall, till it meets the black hair, now somewhat grizzled; dark hazel eyes, full of restless light, that bespeak a quick, irascible temper; the crow's-feet are gathering around the outward angles of the eye-lids, and the sallow jaws show a wrinkle or two; but the man has a good full chest and muscular limbs. You may affirm that the world has not gone altogether wrong with him, though, perhaps, he has had his cares, too, that have scattered the white in his hair, and traced the wrinkle on his face, ere he had passed his fortieth year. And this is Laurence Kennedy, a thriving export merchant in this our good city of Dublin, such as export merchants were sixty years ago. And now look at his *vis-a-vis*. What a mannikin it is! The little fellow, as he sits perched on that high office-stool, in his suit of rusty black, looks more like a jackdaw than a reasonable specimen of the genus "*homo.*" His face is bent down over his book, but you can see enough of it to perceive that it bears a strong affinity in colour to the tallow candle just near it. There, however, the resemblance ceases; the face has none of the smoothness of the candle, for it is diced all over with deep pits, which the smallpox had distributed with a lavish and impartial hand upon every feature. His weak, grey, fringeless eyes are protected with a pair of horn-framed green spectacles, the bow of which is cushioned with a wrapping of green worsted; and as he was never seen without these (it was even said that they mounted guard upon his nose while he slept), Robert Goggin had acquired the *sobriquet* of "Bob Goggles," with his equals, shortened into " Goggles," by his intimate friends and superiors. But who could take upon himself to pronounce upon the age of Goggles? In good faith, you could not venture within a score years of it. He might be under thirty—he might be over sixty. The lean body, and wiry, thin limbs gave you no clue; they would suit equally a hobbledehoy, whose carcase was not yet filled up, or an old man, who was in process of shrivelling. Then you looked in vain to the face.

That cuticle of dead parchment showed no flush of young healthy blood, reddening beneath its surface, no wrinkle or seam of years, where, in a few weeks, Disease had done the work of Time, in the way of ruggedness. There were no whiskers: it might be that they had not come yet; it might be that they had passed away, uprooted by the blight of the variola. Then, as a forlorn hope, you looked at his head: there you were as much at fault as ever, the skull was covered with a bay wig. No doubt, if you chucked off the wig you would find a bald head underneath: but what of that?—the hair of the head might have shared the fate of the whiskers, and so you may as well give the matter up, or rather come to the conclusion that Bob Goggles is, like all unmarried ladies, just of no age in particular. Nevertheless, Bob Goggles has a certain definite age, capable of being expressed by figures, as he would himself demonstrate, and was born upon a particular day and year, more than sixty years before the night upon which we are now looking at him; and for over thirty of those sixty years has he sat upon that self-same stool, in that self-same counting-house; first as clerk to old William Kennedy, and latterly as clerk to Laurence, his son, all that time looking neither younger nor older than he does at this present moment. And there is nobody now who can tell whether he ever looked younger, and nobody can yet divine whether he will ever look older; for they who tended him in infancy, and sported with him in childhood, are all passed away; and they who shall stretch out his little limbs when they are stiffening in death, and gather round him upon the wake-night—God knows who they are—at all events they are not here to answer the question.

And so Kennedy went on thinking, and Goggles went on totting; and all was silent around them, save the ticking of the clock in the hall outside, or the bubbling sound of the bright gas-jet, which now and then streamed out from the seacoal fire, for 'twas a cold, hard wintry night, and the snow had been falling all the day. At length the tones of the neighbouring clock-bell of St. Nicholas's Church rang out ten peals. The sounds seemed to break the thread of the merchant's thoughts; he hitched himself from the wall, brought the stool again upon its four legs, and, reaching down a folio from the shelf near him, he opened it at a particular page, upon the top of which was written, "Laurence Kennedy in account with M—— L——."

"Goggles, how do you make out my account with M—— L——? Look at the entry, will you?"

Goggles made a deprecating movement with his

hand, while he continued his tot. When he had got safe through the column of figures, he paused, and, turning back a few pages, found the required entry.

"Seven hundred and fifty pounds in the Four per cents., and five hundred in Grand Canals."

"All right," said the merchant. "Did you bring out the interest?"

"Yes; on the stock to this, 31st of December. The Canals will give no dividend."

"We'll sell them out, Goggles, and debit myself with the loss. I shouldn't have laid out trust moneys in such security."

"It's no great matter," said the clerk, "I fear you'll never be called to give any account of principal or interest."

"God knows, Goggles: God knows. Ten years— ten long years last midsummer since I placed that money to that account, and all that time I have turned it to the best advantage; and there it is now, nearly doubled, and no one to claim it. Oh, how heavily that sum weighs down upon my heart, like lead. Oh, that I had never retained it! Oh, how gladly would I render it back this night, and so balance this black account, and wipe it from my books and from my conscience ; but it may not be—I fear it may not be."

Goggles laid down his pen gently, and elevated the spectacles from his nose till they rested on his forehead, as a knight of old would throw up the visor of his helmet: 'twas a trick he had, when he was about saying or doing anything emphatic; a symbolical intimation that he was going to use some other organ than his eyes.

"You must not take it so much to heart, Sir; indeed you must not. You have done all that man could do to set things right. Have you not advertised everywhere?—have you not had half the world searched? 'Tis the will of God, Sir; there's no use struggling against the will of God."

"The will of God!" repeated Kennedy, bitterly. "No; not the will of God, but the will of my own hasty, ungovernable temper, that resisted the will of God; that sent her forth a beggar, and defrauded her of her right; when the will of God, had I done it, would have made me just, at all events, ay, and merciful and tender-hearted. Ay, I thrust her out, and she went forth an exile, with my curse upon her; a curse that has returned upon myself tenfold into my bosom. That curse has blighted my hearth, and swept away all my little ones—all but that one poor fragile child; so like *her*, too, that God leaves her to upbraid me with her gentle, uncomplaining face. That curse withers my heart through life, and will weigh upon my soul in the hour of death—weighing it down with the curse of Cain; the curse of that blood that crieth to God out of the ground!"

The merchant buried his face in his hands, and groaned in the bitterness of his spirit. After a moment's silence Goggles gently ventured a word or two of consolation.

"You judge yourself too severely, dear Sir; God knows you do. If you withheld the money, you withheld only what no law could compel you to give. Hasty you were, no doubt, and harsh if you will, but no murderer, neither in thought nor in deed; neither in the sight of God nor man."

Kennedy raised his head, and looked fixedly and sadly upon the face of the little man.

"When I refused her the pittance that should have been her's: when I swore that I would never see or speak to *him* again, she took from her pocket her Bible; her Protestant Bible—and, sobbing and weeping, she read these words to me:—

"'*Whoso hateth his brother is a murderer, and ye*

know that no murderer hath eternal life abiding in him;' and then she laid her hand upon me with such solemn and earnest deprecation, that I shuddered though I did not yield, and she read again:—

"'But whoso hath this world's goods and seeth his brother have need, and shutteth up his bowels of compassion from him, how dwelleth the love of God in him?'

"I remember every word, for they burnt into my brain; but I grew obdurate and incensed, and again I swore that he or his should never dwell beneath the same roof with me."

"It was wrong of you, indeed, Sir, and not what you would have done if you gave your passion time to cool down: but you have repented long and sincerely; you are no murderer, Sir. There will be no such debit against you when the books are made up at the great account."

The merchant shook his head mournfully.

"Tell me, when the Santiago sailed on that luckless voyage from St. Domingo, did she not go down at sea three days after she left the harbour?"

Goggles bowed his head in assent, but was silent. Kennedy continued—

"Did not the ship's register, that was picked up afterwards, tell that amongst the passengers were a poor woman and her child, huddled away somewhere in the fore-cabin, bound for her native land? Was it not her name that I read, till I thought my eyes would burst from their sockets, as I looked at the characters? She and her babe perished! went down, down into that wild desolate ocean—no hand to succour her; no voice to comfort her; with the thought of me and my heartlessness coming, it may be, between her and her prayers to God, and troubling her last moments. Tell me, I say, would she have been in that ship but for me? Would she have found that dreadful grave but for me? No, no; she would not. I am her murderer, indeed!"

Little Goggles' philosophy was neither very deep nor very extensive; he scarce knew what to say in answer to this unwonted burst of passionate remorse. He mounted up into his brain, and searched for some fine casuistical reasoning that might stand to him in the emergency, but in vain; there was nothing of the sort there. Then he dived down into the bottom of his heart, and found something there, which the instinct of love told him was true, though his reason did not come to test it; and so he brought it up and laid it before Kennedy, in his own simple manner.

"I'm not scholar enough, Sir, to contradict your arguments; but I know in my heart you are no murderer. The great and merciful God that brought all these things to pass without your knowledge or design, will not hold you accountable either for the leak in the ship, or the storm on the sea. He will judge you by the intentions of your heart, which are within your own control, and not by the events that are in His own hands to shape. Do you think, Sir, that the priest or the Levite would have been guilty of the death of the poor traveller, if he had perished of his wounds before the good Samaritan came up to relieve him?"

The words of the clerk were words of comfort to his master. They put the matter to him in a light that he was not in the habit of viewing it in. A quick and excitable temperament acting upon a morbid conscience had induced him, as he brooded from day to day, and from year to year, over this most hasty and intemperate act of his life, to deepen its hue to his own mind, till at length, when tidings of the loss of the Santiago reached him some years previously, the shock was so great that his judgment, on this point, became quite warped; and the conviction that he was the murderer of one whom he had, indeed, treated harshly, settled down into the confirmed monomania of his life. Still, this ray of comfort shone in upon him, and calmed him for a moment. A gust of wind was then heard without, and the muffled sound of the heavy snow-shower, falling upon the windows, diverted the thoughts of the two men from the subject which had absorbed them.

"What a wild night it is to close the year with," said Kennedy.

"God help the houseless and the homeless in such a night!" said Goggles.

"Amen, Goggles. And now, I'll leave you for a while, and go up-stairs: 'twill do me good. Meantime, go over to the fire, old fellow, and make yourself comfortable. I'll send you down something warm to help you to find out that error in the tot; and when you have found it let me know, and then we'll balance our books for the old year."

So saying, the merchant rose from his seat and passed from the apartment. Goggles listened to each heavy tread of his master, as he ascended the staircase; then he heard him closing the door of the room overhead, and stepping across the floor, that sounded hollowly beneath his feet. When all was still, the little fellow hopped off his stool, and going over to the fireplace, he gave the coals a modest, timid poke, as though he were taking an unwonted liberty with them: they were of a hot and hasty nature, like their master (and were nothing the worse of that, let me tell you, being coals and not Christians), and so they resisted the assault, gentle as it was, and forthwith broke out into a blaze, and flung their heat at the assailant. Goggles took this retaliation with great complacency, and spread out his cold fingers to receive the first advances: then he rubbed his hands together, and after a little he drew one of the old-fashioned chairs to the fireplace, and taking the account-book from the desk, he sat down cosily before the grate, and with his little feet on the fender, and the folio on his knees, fell once more to work to find out the error in the tot.

CHAPTER II.

THE MISSING FIGURE.

A WILD and dreary night was that 31st of December, 179—. It seemed as if the dying year struggled hard for life to the last. All day long, like poor old Lear, it blustered and raged over its lost empire. All day long, a strong nor'west wind blew keen and bitingly, and the leaden snow-clouds rose thick from the horizon, till they overspread the whole face of heaven, and dimmed the light of the sun that had risen, red and dull, upon the frosty morning. And then, ere noon, the thick, large snow-flakes came down, drifting, with the wind, blindly into the faces of those who traversed the streets, and lying upon window-panes till they well-nigh shut out the dimmed light of day from those within. All day long the snow fell and drifted till, towards night-fall, the streets were covered with a deep, white carpet, over which, now and then, a carriage rolled, with a dull, muffled sound; and on the leeward footways the snow lay piled so deeply that they who passed along were forced to wade half knee-deep through the mass. But when the night fell, the poor old year had well-nigh worn out all his strength; the wind blew but in fitful gusts; the snow-showers were intermittent; the clouds broke up, and through them, as they scudded over the face of heaven, beamed, with her face of placid, heavenly beauty, the moon nearly at her full. Down she looked, sweetly and soothingly, upon that outstretched dying old year, even as sweet Cordelia looked upon the poor old king, "when the great rage was cured in him." And now it is night, wild and dreary, in this our city of Dublin.

There is no more striking picture of desolation than

a city at night, after a heavy fall of snow. No stir, no sound, no life within her. She lies, like a fair, wan corpse in her shroud of snow; her only death-watchers, the silent heavens—her only wake-lights, the moon or stars. Marts, where the din and bustle of commerce resounded through the day: homesteads that rang with a thousand sweet, domestic sounds; doors that poured out their living inmates upon the haunts of life; windows that gleamed with light, as the living eye with "speculation"—all now closed, silent, dark, and dead—so that one looks upwards for relief to heaven from this oppressive sense of death. Oh! glorious and wonderful works of God! Oh! "beauty and mystery" of stars! Ye never sleep or slumber; ever wakeful, like the eye of God; ever, like Him, present, though unseen; like Him, near us, indeed, though hidden in the daytime of brightness and prosperity, but revealing yourselves to light and cheer us in the hour of darkness and trial.

"Bedad, Tim Regan, 'tis the bitterest night that ever I *seen*, God bless it. I'm as cowld as a frog in a spring-well."

"You may say that, Casey," said Regan, poking his head out of his box, as a badger might out of a hole, and then drawing it back again. "I never got such a starving in my born days."

The interlocutors stood at the corner of Trinity-street and College-green. He who first spoke was wrapped up in an ample coat of grey frieze; round his neck was a red worsted comforter which covered his chin and mouth, while his head was comfortably enveloped in a white cotton nightcap surmounted by a round hat, the former drawn down in front, almost to his eyes, and leaving only these organs and a red nose exposed to the weather. The cuffs of his coat were brought together, so as to protect, as with a muff, his hands from the cold; his right arm clasped close to his breast a long pole, with a pike and a hook at the end of it, contrived as well to arrest those who fled from the nocturnal authority, as to assail those who resisted it, and a rattle was stuck in the belt that surrounded his waist. Close to where he stood was a box, or, as it was familiarly termed in the slang of the day, a "bulk," secured against the wall of the house, and so formed, that the sides and roof, which closed by day, opened out and afforded a shelter from the weather by night. Within this the other speaker was ensconced, in a similar attire to his companion, while his pike lay against the side of the watch-box. These two worthies constituted part of the civic guard of Dublin, to whom the fortunes of the town were nightly committed. They were, for the most part, superannuated servants or followers of the Lords Mayor, and other great functionaries of Dublin, who thus provided for them at the public expense; and as they were able to do little, they did it accordingly with all their hearts. As peaceful men, they felt it their duty to set a good example to their fellow-citizens; and, therefore, made it a point to sleep through the night, the only interruption to which excellent practice arose from the necessity, somewhat unreasonably imposed upon them, of crying the hours. This annoyance was, however, greatly diminished by an arrangement amongst themselves, whereby one of their number kept the watch each hour, while the rest betook themselves to repose with such earnestness, that to "sleep as sound as a watchman" became a proverb to express a state of the most profound somnolency. It was now Casey's hour of watching; and as his period of vigil was nearly ended, he had waked up the sleepy Regan a short time before the moment when we first made their acquaintance. In a moment Regan turned out of his den, and the two old men, with slow and drowsy step, proceeded on their beat towards the College, chatting as they went along. If a Pythagorean had just then seen them, in their grey attire and white polls, as they gossipped with one another, he might have fancied that the souls of the geese that saved the Capitol had migrated into the bodies of these old fellows; and that, true to the instinct of their nature, they still cackled and waddled over the sleeping city. And now upon the ear of night the clock of the old Post Office pealed forth the hour of eleven. More distinctly, and in deeper tones, the record of Time's flight was taken up by the bells of Christ Church; then the neighbouring Church of St. Nicholas Within-the-Walls gave its notes of warning; next the chiming tongues of St. Patrick's bells spoke the message; and, ere these had ceased, the far-away voice of the bell-clock of Madame Stevens' Hospital took up the challenge; and so from one to the other these chroniclers of old Time passed the fleeting hour upon his way, till they had fairly sent him out of the city, through the silent parks, and along the sweet valley of the Liffey. And onward, onward went that flying hour, staying but a moment with each, on his westward journey, ever irrevocable to those he had passed.

Meantime, the city watchmen were not idle. Though all other thieves might steal without challenge or interruption during the hours of night, they took good care that the great thief, Time, should not filch even one hour from the world without an outcry.

"Pa-a-st e-le-ven!" sung out Casey, with all the power of his lungs. "Pa-a-st e-le-ven!" repeated Regan, taking for a moment the short pipe from his mouth, with whose fumes he was comforting himself. "Pa-a-st e-le-ven!" was echoed along the snowy streets, throughout the city, from bulk to bulk, as nightcapped heads were thrust out. Many a lightly-sleeping maiden was waked from her pleasant dream. Many a sleepless sick man, tossing on his bed of fever, heard that vociferation, and gave his malediction to the senseless noise that came so suddenly upon him, making his heart beat and his brow throb with pain. Many a housebreaker and night-prowler laughed as he heard the clamour, for he knew that in five minutes more most of those conservators of the city would be snoring in their boxes, and that the few who were on their beats would be as unconscious as somnambulists.

Just then the voices of some drunken revellers, trolling a snatch of a drinking-song, broke upon the repose into which the city was again settling down after the clamorous interruption of the watchmen. The sounds came from near the northern wing of the College: then some words of parley and altercation, mixed with laughter, followed, and the next moment the shrill cry of a woman's voice pierced the air,

The cry was that of one seemingly in distress; and so piteous and appealing was its tone, that the two watchmen ran forward to the spot with the best speed they could command.

"Them's the College-boys at their divilmint, I'll be bound," said Regan, dashing the red tobacco from his pipe, and grasping his pike valiantly.

"Like enough," responded Casey; "there's neither peace nor quiet night or day through the means of 'em. One would think they might be tired for once, after the pelting of snowballs they gave the Ormond boys this evening. Lord save us! do you hear that again?" as another shriek smote on the air: "hurry, man, or there'll be murder."

In another moment they were at the place whence the sounds proceeded. Close to the railings of the College were three young men dressed in the extreme fashion of the day, with hair in exquisite buckle and profusely powdered. They were evidently gentlemen, with which character it was not then deemed inconsistent to be in the state of most unequivocal drunkenness in which these youths were. Two of them were linked together, with their backs to the railings, laughing heartily at the third, who, with his arms round the waist of a woman, was addressing her with an air of maudlin gallantry, and with as much gravity as his drunkenness enabled him to command. He had just concluded some speech, in which the words "Incomparable paragon of loveliness—beautiful Venus—divinely frigid Diana," and a profession of eternal devotion, were alone intelligible. The woman struggled hard for freedom.

"Oh, Sir, if you be a gentleman, as you look to be, for the love of God suffer me to pass. You would not surely molest an unprotected woman?"

"Molest! Madam, upon my honour, and 'fore Gad, you may depend on me. I only want to protect you from these wild young fellows. This, you see, madam, is Buck O'Reilly, and this is Fagan, one of 'the Mohawks;'" and with his disengaged hand he essayed an introduction of his two compotators. "Fagan, my dear madam, is one of the most desperate Mohawks in existence," he continued in a confidential whisper.

The two others broke out into an uproarious fit of laughter.

"Bravo, Lucas! Go it, my Cherokee! Pray don't mind us! We're in no hurry, you know, quite at your service."

"Hands off, hands off, Sir!" said Regan, pushing in between the men. "Let go the woman; don't you see she has no mind for your civilities?"

"Down with the Charlie; pink the cursed old bulkey," cried the Buck and the Mohawk, endeavouring to disengage their swords from the scabbards.

"Be quiet, be quiet, gentlemen," said Casey, who saw that he had to deal with men too drunk to make any effective resistance, "unless you want to spend the night in the watchhouse."

The two men rushed furiously at Casey. The Buck came to the ground before he reached his opponent, while the Mohawk pitched heavily, like a log, into the old watchman, well-nigh bearing him down by his drunken weight. Meantime, Lucas, releasing the woman, attacked Regan, who, valiantly springing his rattle, received the enemy with his pike-handle grasped in both his hands. From all quarters watchmen came hobbling up, springing their rattles till the air was filled with the discordant creaking. The three gentlemen were speedily reduced, and surrounded by twice as many watchmen.

"I say, Charlie, my old fellow," said Lucas, who seemed to be less *game* than his companions, "'twas all a mistake, you see. I thought the lady was a particular friend of mine, and I was only going to take care of her home; so here's something for your trouble;" and he slipped a crown into Regan's ready hand.

"That's just what I was thinking, your honour, when I made bould to set you right. A real gentleman is always ready to listen to reason;" and he gave a significant look to his fellows, intimating that matters were adjusted in the way in which watchmen always found it their account to settle them with all but poor rogues who had no money in their pockets.

"And a real gentleman is always ready to make up to a poor fellow for breaking his ribs," said Casey, groaning with the affectation of internal suffering.

This appeal was responded to by the Mohawk, who, considering it complimentary to his personal prowess to have *smashed* the Charlie, was disposed to be generous. And so the three *gentlemen* staggered onwards, heaven knows whither; and the watchmen went off, no doubt to drink; and the half-dozen homeless, miserable wretches who, on that bleak winter's night, were the spectators of the scene, wandered away; but the woman, where was she? No one looked for her—no one thought of her—no one had seen her since she was freed from the arm of the drunken "Cherokee."

The moon broke out from the ragged clouds that scudded across her orb, and shone with full splendour upon the outspread city that lay beneath her. There in that area, wherein were congregated all the memorials of the genius, the eloquence, the patriotism, the learning of Ireland, the beams of the full moon shone down in her cold glory. Shining far away in the eastern heavens, she left the façade of Trinity College in deep shadow—a shadow that projected far into "the Green" the outlines of the central pile and pavilions of the University. But the light struck clear and strong upon the beautiful mass of buildings that formed the northern side of College-green. One by one, the graceful shafts of those Ionic pillars of pure white marble rose from their bases, casting their shadows into the circular colonnade that ran round the eastern side of the mass. To the south, a deep recess formed a court-yard, along three sides of which the colonnade was continued. A portion of this was left in darkness, but the moonbeams flooded over the roof, and fell upon the façade that fronted the east, and lit it up in a grand and solemn lustre, while the partial rays glinted upon the southern front, and brought out, between the shadows of the columns, the principal entrance to the building. And the whole pile rose upon the sight, massive, colossal, vast and symmetrical—a building, whose exterior may challenge competition with the finest structures of Greece and Italy—within whose walls were heard the voices of the most eloquent men of their age—Grattan and Flood, Plunket and Bushe—men who have made for Irish oratory and Irish genius a name throughout the world. Such was the Irish House of Parliament at the close of the last century! The *genius loci* has long since fled from the spot, and the spirit of commerce has fixed her empire in those halls which once resounded with the eloquence of the senator, and echoed the wit and brilliant sallies of the orator. A mighty change, indeed: but let him who mourns over the altered destinies of our land remember that Ireland's strength lies in a thorough and hearty union with her elder sister, in a participation of all her greatness, and a generous and earnest emulation of her in all the arts that elevate a nation, and raise a people in the estimation of mankind.

Upon the steps of the western colonnade of the Parliament House sat one in whose heart rose no thoughts of the beauty and the glory around her. Full of sorrow, indeed, were the meditations of her mind; home memories, before which an angry spirit stood, forbidding her heart's access, even as the cherubim stood with flaming sword between Paradise and our first parents; thoughts of those beloved in childhood, cherished in youth, estranged ere that youth had well-nigh passed. Where were they now? Would they receive her?—would they love her as in the days of old? As she pondered over these things, the woman groaned in her anguish, and cried aloud—

"Be thou not far from me, O Lord, my strength, haste Thee to help me."

With the prayer on her lips, she raised her eyes to heaven.

"Mistress, you're a stranger in Dublin, I'm thinking. If I can be of any assistance to you, you're heartily welcome to my services."

He who addressed her was the watchman that rescued her from the drunken "Cherokee."

"I am, indeed, a stranger," said the woman, "and would gladly accept your kindness. Will you give me your protection to Nicholas-street?"

"'Tis beyond my beat a long way," said Regan, "howsomever, I'll not leave you to walk the streets alone so far this hour of night. So come along, in the name of God."

The woman arose and moved forward. The watchman walked by her side respectfully. There was that about her that showed him she was one who, poor though she seemed, knew no degradation beyond that of poverty. And so they passed along the silent and snow-covered footway, down through Dame-street, and up Cork-hill, by the Gate of the Castle, and along the Castle-street, passing by the Rose Tavern, still a thriving establishment, and, not many years previously, the resort of many of the distinguished social and political clubs of the city. Then they entered the Skinners-row, a narrow street which has since been made wide and spacious, under the name of Christchurch-place. At that time it was not much over seventeen feet in breadth; but, though mean in appearance, it was the residence of many of the wealthiest jewellers and goldsmiths of the city. At its south-western extremity stood a massive building of hewn stone, two stories high. The moon's light shone slantingly upon its front, and displayed two antique figures in robes and periwigs: this was the Tholsel, round which they turned into Nicholas-street, lying in the shadow of the night, for the moonbeams shining from the east could not find their way into it, and the dim and flickering oil-lamp shed but a faint and partial light around.

"Now, mistress," said Regan, "you're in Nicholas-street. There's the church, and farther on is Kennedy-court. What house are you seeking?"

The woman hesitated for a moment. She seemed to be struggling with some feelings that ultimately got the better of her. At length she said, with some embarrassment—

"I will not trespass on you any farther. I can now find the house I want. I am very thankful for your kindness. I wish I could show my gratitude as fully as I feel it."

She held forth in her hand a silver coin. The old watchman shook his head, and said—

"No, no, mistress. I can afford to do a good turn for nothing; besides, that drunken young scapegrace paid me well enough already on your account. I have a wife myself, and daughters too, for that matter: and for their sakes I can help a friendless woman, and so good-night, and God protect you. I must hurry back to be on my beat to sing out 'all's well' when the inspector goes his rounds."

Then the watchman retraced his steps, and was soon out of sight round the corner of the Tholsel. The woman passed on rapidly a few paces, then she stopped at a doorway on the left side of the street. A projecting oil-lamp burned muddily over the heavy stone pediment, and gave her light enough to see a massive brass knocker. She lifted it hurriedly and knocked with a trembling hand. The sound reverberated through the still air and smote upon her heart with a sudden shock. A thousand memories were evoked by that sound. Hopes, fears, doubts, agonies crowded upon her: they were too much for a frame weakened by illness, and nerves shaken by the events of the evening; and, ere her summons was answered, she sank down unconscious in the snow that lay upon the steps.

CHAPTER III.

THE TOT SET RIGHT.

WHEN she who had wandered through the midnight snows and sunk on the cold door-steps opened her eyes, and became once again conscious, she was as one waking from a long dream. Years, occupied by that dream, vanished, and she gazed around on familiar objects. The room and its quaint orderly furniture were those of her childhood. There was the curtained window at which she had stood by day, the bright cheery hearth at which she had sat by night. The chimney-glass in its antique frame, with the peacock's feathers at each side. The old clock ticked upon the mantelpiece. The green parrot swung upon his hoop in the gilded cage. And kneeling beside her, one chafed her temples, and kissed her cold hands, with all the gentle kindness which it is the blessed gift of woman alone to minister. And there, too, bent over her, one whose eyes were full of awe and wonder, of unutterable love and tenderness, of joy and sorrow, hope and doubt, strangely blended.

"Are you my own dear Mary, alive and in the flesh? or are you her blessed spirit come to summon me to my last dread account? Speak, in the name of God's own mother, I adjure you."

"Laurence, dear Laurence, I am your own sister Mary. God has spared me life to come back and throw myself upon your love."

The man smote his breast with his open palms, and heaved a mighty sigh: 'twas the heaving of a heart that cast off for ever a load that was dragging it down to the grave.

"Then I am no murderer! O Lord, I thank thee;" and flinging himself down on his knees beside the couch, he kissed her poor, pale forehead and her cold lips again and again, and wept and laughed by turns, while that gentle sister clasped his head in her wasted hands, and soothed him, and blest him, and wept with him; till at last the other woman, fearing that the excitement would injure both, rose up, and with quiet, yet firm restraint, drew the man away.

"Dear husband, you must compose yourself, for

her sake as well as for your own. See how weak and faint she is, you will surely injure her. Come," and she led him to a chair apart, and then returned as quietly as before to the suffering one, and busied herself again in tending her, saying little, but doing all things needful. And the man looked on the while, wonderingly and musingly, yet not daring to speak, keeping closed the flood-gates of his feelings lest they should break out again, and overwhelm him. And, after a little time, they were all more composed and tranquil, and Mary spoke for a time in a low voice with Mrs. Kennedy, and then she arose and tasted, in thankfulness, of the food that was set before her, and drank of the old Spanish wine, which her father had loved, and would give to her, as a child, on festive occasions. And then they sat by the fireside, that long-severed, long-estranged brother and sister, her hand in his hand, her head upon his breast. And the quiet, gentle wife, she had stolen noiselessly away out of the room, leaving the two together, while they poured out their hearts in mutual explanations.

"Yes; dear Mary, from the hour when I snatched my hand from you, as you supplicated me upon your knees, and I passed out through that door, with reproaches on my lips and bitterness in my heart, I have known no peace. Ere one week had passed, I sought for you at *his* lodgings, everywhere, but you were not to be found; you were both gone, nobody knew whither."

"We left the country the day after that bitter parting. Why should we stay where we were outcasts and beggars?"

"I sought for you everywhere; I advertised in the papers here and in England. I made inquiries through my correspondents abroad, but in vain; no answer, no clue, and yet you must have seen them, Mary. Was this well done, sister? You were not used to have an unrelenting spirit."

"Yes; I did see what you put in the papers copied into a foreign journal; and oh! dear Laurence, God knows how my heart yearned towards you; but *he* would not suffer me to reply. The wounds you had inflicted on his pride and honour were still rankling. You had called him, he told me, a beggar and an adventurer. You accused him of abusing your confidence and hospitality; of clandestinely seducing your sister's affections; of making a base and ungrateful return for your bounty. What bounty, save the money that he earned by his own honest toil? Oh! brother, brother! you know not the man you so accused."

x

The woman raised her head from where it had been resting, and a flush spread over her pallid face. It might have been anger, it might have been but pride; whatever was its cause, it soon passed away. That meek soul had been too severely schooled by the world's trials, too deeply taught by God's chastisements, to cherish the one or the other emotion: and so she laid her head once again lovingly upon her brother's breast.

"I did all that you say, Mary, nor do I now seek to justify it altogether: but when you judge my conduct, do not forget how sorely I was tried—tried in all that was dearest to my heart, my affections, my religion, my pride, my name."

The woman shook her head mournfully, but made no reply. It might be that she knew how her brother had felt all these things, though she could not admit that they should have tried him so severely.

"Bear with me for a little while, dear sister," he continued, "while for once I lay bare before you my my heart and my motives. Even should it pain you, still you will not deny me the opportunity of pleading my own cause. When I shall have done this, my lips shall be closed on the subject for ever. Condemn me then as you will. God knows you cannot condemn me as much as my own conscience does.

"Of all his children, you and I alone were left to our dear father. How he loved you, you know well: but he loved you not more dearly than I did, when on his death-bed he commended you to my care. I watched over you, Mary, more as a father would do than a brother. You were the light of my home, and the pride of my heart, and I sought for no other companion while I had you, no other mistress for my house. And so passed on many a happy year till you were a full-grown woman; and then came the shadow over our bright life."

The merchant paused, as if half afraid to proceed. At length he took courage and resumed.

"One morning I received from a Bourdeaux correspondent a letter requesting my good offices in favour of a French Protestant who had been forced to leave his native land. I remember, as if it were but yesterday, the bearer of that letter. 'Twas Joseph Le Maistre. I pitied him; for I hated in my heart all persecution for conscience sake. My house was opened to him; I procured him tuitions as a teacher of languages, and I suffered him to make you perfect in the knowledge of his native tongue. Oh! Mary, my own sister! was it honourable, was it generous, that he should creep in between our hearts; that he should rob me of your love; that he should estrange your heart from its duty, and your soul from the religion of your fathers? And yet all this he did, Mary; and I suspected nothing of it, till one and the same day I learned that you were a Protestant, and the wife of Le Maistre."

"All this my husband did, Laurence; yet was he neither ungenerous nor dishonourable. If there be cause for blame, and I do not deny it, let that blame rest where it should, upon me. My love for my dear husband I have never for a moment repented of; in my changed faith, I humbly rejoice. I do not, and I never did, justify my marriage without your knowledge; *he* would have had it otherwise, but I overruled him; for I knew your quick temper and your strong attachment to your faith, and I feared that you would prevent our union. Dearly have we paid the penalty, when you sent me forth fortuneless upon the world; I know you had the right legally to do so, for my portion was made subject to my marrying with your consent."

"And every farthing of that portion I placed to your credit, and will account to you honestly for it and all its fruits."

"Oh! brother, this is indeed being more than just, it is generous; generous and good as my own dear brother was wont to be in our young days.

This will enable us all to be independent, will save us from the sharp pang and degradation of poverty—*him* and my child."

Kennedy started involuntarily. Up to this moment he had not thought of the existence of Joseph Le Maistre; somehow he had concluded that he was dead.

"He, your husband! Did he not die before you left St. Domingo? His name was not amongst those in the registry of the Santiago."

"He was not in the Santiago. He had sailed a week before in a vessel bound for Barbadoes, where he had friends on whose aid he relied. There we were to meet him when the Santiago should touch on her voyage to Europe. I will not relate to you the terrors of that dreadful night, when our ship went down so suddenly that the sleepers were awakened to rush on deck and find their graves in the sea; nor how, as I sank with the vessel in the seething waters that sucked us downwards, with my arms round my child, I thought of you, brother, and prayed God to forgive us both."

The merchant groaned. He called to mind the picture that his distempered fancy drew of that awful scene, and how different it was from the reality. The woman continued:

"Some friendly hand threw me a rope. I seized it, and was drawn, with my child, into a small boat. There were but two men in it. All that dreadful night we drifted about; and when the light of the morning broke, they discovered a ship not a mile distant. One of the men took my shawl, and raising it up on an oar, signalled the vessel. After some time she perceived us, and in half-an-hour more we were on board, and in safety. We were landed at St. Lucia, and I contrived from that to make my way to Barbadoes, and found my husband. There we remained many years, and at last we have sought my native city; for I had a strong belief that God would not will that we should be thus estranged for ever. And I said I would seek you once again, and humble myself before you, my own dear brother."

"Nay, dear sister, not so; you shall not humble yourself to me, for I, too, have erred; but you shall lie in my heart as closely as you did before. When you left me, Mary, my house was lonely, and I sought one to solace me in my sorrow, and such a one I found in my dear wife, your old playmate Hester. She will be to you as a sister, and you shall share our home—you and your little one."

"Laurence, there is *one* whom you do not name.

I share no home and no heart in which he also is not a sharer. Whither he goes, I go. His people shall be my people, as his God is my God."

The woman paused, and looked anxiously at her brother for a reply; but no reply came. His brow grew dark. The evil spirit was upon him—that spirit of anger against the husband of his sister, which years of suffering had not subdued. He rose hastily from his seat, and paced the room with rapid steps. Oh! poor, frail, human nature—the slave of sin and passion! With all the light that shines upon you from above, still loving the darkness; with the voice of God speaking to you everywhere and in everything, still closing your ear as the deaf adder; with countless unseen pitying angels around you, ever striving to bear you in their hands, and raise you heavenward, still grovelling in the dust. There, in that man's heart, was then going on one of those mysterious spiritual battles which, from the first hour of the first man's fall till the last hour of the last man's life, have been, and shall be, waged; the good and the evil striving for the mastery, as Michael and the Devil contended for the body of Moses. And the battle is fierce, and the fortune of the fight shifts and wavers; but at last 'tis over, and the evil angels are masters of the human battle-field for a season, and enter in, and possess it.

Kennedy stopped short before her.

"I wronged you, and I am ready to make all reparation, sister, in my power to you. *Him* I never wronged, but he has sorely wronged me. Let us be as we are, strangers for ever. I swore that it should be so. Shall I break my solemn oath?"

Mary Le Maistre rose from her seat, pale as death, yet composed as one who had taken a fixed resolve.

"Laurence Kennedy, for the last time, farewell! Your hasty and violent temper I knew well, and I did not cease to love you, even when that temper wrought me sorrow and suffering; but I did not know till now that you had so unforgiving a spirit. To-night I left my husband without his knowledge, while he slept after a heavy day of toil, and alone, in this cold winter's night, I sought your house—with what hopes it is idle now to say. Well, well, these hopes have failed me. I will return to my husband, and we will pray that you may never plead in vain for that forgiveness which you refused to another."

She moved towards the door, but Kennedy stepped between it and her.

"Mary, Mary, for the love of God do not leave me!"

"The love of God! What do you know of the love of God, or how do you dare to appeal to it? God loves the vilest soul that sins against him, and pardons him. That love is not in you, Laurence Kennedy. 'If a man say I love God, and hateth his brother, he is a liar.'"

The words fell upon the ear of Kennedy with a terrible and solemn force, and pierced his heart as it were with a sword. The memory of that scene years ago, when last they stood together in that very room, even as they did now, face to face, came vividly before him; and the words which she had then spoken sounded again as distinctly in his ears as they did that day — an awful denunciation and appeal to God against him. Once more the life-battle is renewed in his soul, and the Word of God, quick and sharp as a two-edged sword, drives back the evil angels till they have but one stronghold left.

"My oath — my solemn oath!" cried the man, perplexed and in agony. "If I had not taken that oath ———"

"Think you, Laurence Kennedy, that you can plead that oath against Christ's command to love your brother, when you and that brother shall stand, at the last day, before His judgment-seat? Look round and answer me that question."

Mechanically he turned his head in the direction to which she pointed. There stood the man of whom they spoke, as if summoned by some mysterious power to confront him now in the presence of an unseen God, as he should yet do before his visible Judge. A slight, small man, on whose delicate face the lines of sorrow were prematurely traced, with a dull, languid eye, from which all the playful light of bygone days had vanished. There was no pride now in that form, somewhat bent with a habitual stoop; and as Kennedy looked at him, he could have fancied that half-a-century had passed over that man since last they met. He stood meekly, yet with a manly and composed dignity, just within the doorway, awaiting the advance of his wife's brother. Kennedy stood irresolute and motionless—the battle rages within him— the stronghold of pride and long-cherished anger is sore assailed, but is not yet taken.

"Dear husband," said his wife, in her quiet yet constraining accents, "Mr. Le Maistre has come with me from his lodging this wild winter night to see *you*. Will you not receive and welcome him—Mary's husband, Laurence?"

The little girl, who had accompanied her father when she heard the name, stepped softly up and looked into her uncle's face, with a sweet smile and a look of childish wonder, and touching his hand, said—

"Are you my Uncle Laurence, that papa taught me to name in my prayers night and morning?"

The battle is won, the stronghold is carried, and the evil ones are driven from it for ever. Out of the mouth of the babe has God ordained the strength that gave the victory. Kennedy raised the little one in his arms and kissed her, and then setting her gently down, held out his hand to Le Maistre—

"Come in, brother Le Maistre; come in and sit down with us. With my whole heart I make you welcome."

The women wept silently, but the child shouted gleefully and clapped her hands. She was fresher from heaven than they, and her spiritual sensations were yet akin to those of the angels; like them, she rejoiced over the sinner that had repented.

After a little time, the door was opened, and a head thrust hesitatingly into the room.

"What the devil is wrong now?" asked Kennedy impatiently.

He felt half-ashamed that any one except those around him should witness his emotion.

"There's nothing wrong now, Sir, but all's right; and it was not the devil at all, but a figure that was left out in the last entry in your own private account, and so I put it down to your credit; and all's right now, and the books balance to a farthing."

"Come in, Goggles—come in, old fellow; all *is* right, thank God, in my accounts with the whole world. See, here are old friends; won't you wish them a happy new year?"

Goggles obeyed the summons, and walked up to the fireplace, where they were all sitting.

"Lord save us! who's this at all? Blessed Virgin! it cannot be! Yes, but it is. Ah, dear Miss Mary— I beg your pardon, Mistress Le Maistre. Is it possible?—alive, alive as sure as two and two's four. Mr. Le Maistre, I'm proud to see you once again. Ah, Sir, you've been at *the multiplication table*, I see, since you left us;" and the old man gave a low chuckle as he looked at the child.

Goggles was a wag in a small way, but his *jeux d'esprit* and figures were always arithmetical.

"Ay, and a great *addition* to their happiness, Goggles," said his master, humouring the old man's foible.

"He! he! he! Very true, Sir. Thank God, there's an end to the *long division*, at all events."

"Sit down, old friend, you shall share in my joy as you have known my sorrow. Come, drink the health of our friends here in a glass of wine, and wish them a happy new year."

As he spoke, the bells of St. Patrick's Church rang out a jocund peal upon the night. The old year had passed away—passed with all its sins and its sorrows, all its good and its evil—passed away from Time into Eternity—gone to be written up in God's register, against the last day of accounting, when Time itself shall be no more. And one bright entry will appear under the head of that old year of 179—, the record of pride subdued, of anger overcome by love, of estranged hearts united; and whatever sins were registered in the page of that year against any of those who then sat lovingly together at its close, I well believe that the earnest repentance of that last half-hour will be availing with a merciful Judge, and that the finger of God's love will set that repentance and sorrow and suffering against the pride and enmity and anger, and so balance that account at the great day of reckoning.

"That's all true," Mr. Slingsby, I make no doubt," said the Professor, in his own dry way.

"As true, Mr. Chubble," I replied, "as the tale you once told us of your friend Dick Woodenspoon and his marriage."

"Hem! I thought as much."

"I don't care a pipe-stopper," said old Freke, "whether it be true or not. It has put us over an hour pleasantly enough."

"A very good criticism," said Uncle Saul.

"And one," I added, "whose spirit I recommend to all critics, from those of the quarterly reviews to the half-penny newspapers."

THE END.

www.ingramcontent.com/pod-product-compliance
Lightning Source LLC
Chambersburg PA
CBHW030743230426
43667CB00007B/826